The Impassioned Soul

Pursuing Christ With a Holy Obsession

Morton Bustard

Destiny Image® Publishers, Inc.
P.O. Box 310
Shippensburg, PA 17257-0310

"Speaking to the Purposes of God for this Generation
and for the Generations to Come"

ISBN 0-7684-2113-6

(Originally published as *Passion for His Presence*
by Impart Publishing under ISBN 0-9669235-0-2)

For Worldwide Distribution
Printed in the U.S.A.

This book and all other Destiny Image, Revival Press, MercyPlace, Fresh Bread, Destiny Image Fiction, and Treasure House books are available at Christian bookstores and distributors worldwide.

For a U.S. bookstore nearest you, call **1-800-722-6774**.
For more information on foreign distributors, call **717-532-3040**.
Or reach us on the Internet: **www.reapernet.com**.

Dedication

Dedicated to my loving mother, Beatrice Helen Bustard, whose unwavering walk with the Lord impacted my life more than any other has. I am a composite of numerous ministries that have assisted in tutoring and developing my own ministry, to whom I am ever indebted. However, with no disrespect intended, Mother's influence remains incomparable.

Due to numerous errors in the initial edition of this book, I am reprinting it with a new title, *The Impassioned Soul*. In the process, Mother was promoted to her heavenly home, November 9, 1999. However, she was able to see the book I am so honored to dedicate to her.

Mother's consistency through life's journey afforded me strength for the miles that lie ahead. Her maternal nurturing embraced excellence and her spirituality demonstrated Godliness. If I were asked to select a word to adequately characterize this precious lady, *faithful* would win unanimously.

Mother, thanks a million for everything. You were the most unselfish person I know. Your exemplary life reminds me that, whatever goodness I possess, I am a small chip off the block. You had a titanium constitution, lightweight yet uncompromising, with maximum efficiency.

Probably the greatest lesson you taught me is that we do not have a millisecond to squander on self-pity. In your early teenage years you were obligated to take up heavy responsibilities with the passing of your mother. Your burden never lightened but at times increased considerably. Whenever your hopes were eclipsed by despair, you patiently waited for a brighter day. A new dawn has now broken.

Acknowledgments

Jesus Christ—For allowing access into an intimate relationship with you. I would be a fool not to pursue such an opportunity.

My wife, Marilyn, and my daughters, Datha and Kayla—Thanks for enduring and understanding my temperament as I labored to finish the book. You three gals are what my life on earth is all about.

Rev. Dan Rigdon—Thank you for the Introduction as well as the compassionate care you employ as a shepherd. Your people skills are unparalleled.

Rev. T.F. Tenney, Abundant Life Church—You are blessed with some of the finest saints God ever did make. Thanks for opening your doors and arms to my family. We appreciate you more than you know.

Elizabeth Allen—You are patience personified. You are as thoughtful as you are professional.

Endorsement

The Impassioned Soul is an important work that should be read by anyone who is seeking a genuine encounter with God. Few people ever write a book that has the ability to turn the soul of man toward his Creator with a thirst for His presence. Fewer still write a book where the author's passion is so authentic and evident that you know he has heard from God. The chapter "Precious Pain" so affected my life that it inadvertently wove its way into my preaching. Now the world will know what I know—Morton Bustard writes from his experiences in the presence of the Lord. This is an important work!

Tommy Tenney
Author, GodChaser

Contents

Foreword

Morton Bustard is an anointed man of God. He has had a life-changing effect on countless individuals as he travels internationally with a trans-mobile prophetic ministry. Now he has taken up pen and paper, and the resulting work is as uniquely anointed as the writer.

In its original form, the title was *Passion for His Presence*. That phrase is the answer to what sets the book and its author apart from the rest. Morton Bustard's passionate pursuit of the presence of God is what facilitates the free flow of timeless truth from chapter to chapter. From "The Restricted Zone"—where he reminds us that "Regardless of where we are in our walk with God at the present time, we can advance toward Him and be as close as we choose. There are no limitations barring us from a deeper relationship"—to the closing story of Hagar (and his personal testimony of a desert experience), the author invites the reader to catch a glimpse of the Savior, to become an *impassioned soul*. Time and again, using familiar stories from the Scripture, he issues this challenge: "Vacant prayer closets must be revisited and not abandoned until Heaven has issued a statement."

The Impassioned Soul by Morton Bustard will prove to be one of those books you read again and again. It expresses the author's holy obsession while triggering the reader's hunger for the presence of God. In his own unique and lyrical writing style, Morton Bustard captures the spirit of an individual who is committed above all else to pursuing Christ in every aspect of his life. He is not trafficking in unfelt truth. Every chapter has been born in the crucible of his own personal experience. It will challenge you. It will change you. You will find yourself renewing your own magnificent obsession with Jesus Christ; you will become an *impassioned soul* and share in the holy obsession.

T.F. Tenney

Introduction

It was in 1989 that the saints at Abundant Life Church were first blessed with the anointed ministry of Brother Morton Bustard. Three years and several meetings later, we invited him and his good family to move to Plano, Texas, become our resident evangelist, and base his international ministry out of our church. This decision we have never had reason to regret. In our case, familiarity has not bred contempt. Through the years our respect for Morton and the sincerity from which he speaks have continued to grow. His life has been able to pass the scrutiny of close relationship. The man and his message are one.

The title of this offering, *The Impassioned Soul*, could easily be a most concise yet complete description of the central desire of the author's soul. The chapters freely flow from his heart into ours. While revealing much about his own attitude toward his relationship with God, they also point us to the riches resident in the Master's presence and generously appropriated for those who are passionate about finding a place of fellowship at His side.

As you ruminate on the timeless truths so powerfully presented in these "chapters with a message," you will find yourself challenged, encouraged, and enlightened. The cracked earth of the parched soul whose passion has waned will experience the movement of new life. The dying embers of a one-time passion to know the Lord in both the power of the resurrection and the fellowship of His sufferings will again flame in the glory of the pursuit of high spiritual attainment. Those presently on the road will no doubt find themselves to be kindred spirits with the author and be the recipients of much needed understanding concerning the ardors of their current journey. All will sense that the author knows that of which he speaks and be prompted to persevere.

Near the end of the first chapter of this book there is a simple yet most heartening profundity: "The die was cast; the precedent was established; we can come as close to Christ as we desire." How wonderful it is that our Lord has thrown wide the door of equal opportunity for whosoever will to enter into the inner sanctum of sacred relationship. How close I want to be is entirely up to me. Anyone possessing the passion can know the fulfillment of living in His presence. The realization of this dream is within our reach.

There is no privileged zone that is declared off limits to the serious and sincere soul who seeks. No less than the Lord Himself has given the assurance that such should surely find.

Dan L. Rigdon, Senior Pastor
Abundant Life Church
Plano, Texas

Chapter One

The Restricted Zone

He that dwelleth in the secret place of the most High
shall abide under the shadow of the Almighty.
Psalm 91:1

Singapore is without doubt one of the most beautiful cities I have ever visited. Climate-wise and architecturally speaking, one cannot ask for more. And, in my experience, the people there are more than friendly and very accommodating.

I had the privilege of ministering in Singapore on two different occasions. Each time I was treated with amicable hospitality, and I look forward to returning someday.

On my first visit, the missionary kindly gave my small evangelistic party a tour of the city. As we made our way toward the downtown area, I noticed an illuminated sign that read this: "Restricted Zone."

The missionary explained the purpose for the sign. The business district is located there, and it is a place where important decisions are made and millions of dollars change hands every few minutes. The civil engineers zoned the area as "restricted" in order to avoid congested traffic in this extremely vital section of Singapore. However,

1

anyone is permitted to enter if they are willing to pay the price. A daily pass is required in order to have access.

Unlike this area in Singapore, all of humanity is a candidate for entrance into the Kingdom of God, regardless of skin color, nationality, or status in society. Any doctrine that suggests otherwise is not biblically sound.

The opportunity to become a child of God is available to all. The requisite does not involve money or theological degrees from acclaimed seminaries. Submitting blood samples, enduring physical examinations, and visiting a consulate to acquire a visa are not necessary. The stipulation for entrance into the Kingdom is simply this: *You must be born again* (see Jn. 3:7).

The veil in the temple, which restrained all except the high priest from entering the Holy of Holies, has been *rent in two* (see Mt. 27:51). No longer are just a privileged few permitted to enter. The veil hangs severed; the arms of the Lord are open to accept those who heed His call.

Once we enter the Kingdom of God, we must decide how close we want to get to the King. Will we be content to live as subjects in a vast domain who never view the inside of the throne room? Or will we seek every opportunity to establish an intimate relationship with the Lord?

Christ's Kingdom is unique from any other. What other royal family permits peasants to live in the palace? People whose pasts are blemished with infractions, regardless of how disreputable, are not prohibited from touching Him.

Unlike other sovereigns, Jesus is accessible to all who desire His company. There are no appointments required or time restrictions imposed. And frequently this King approaches us, desiring our companionship.

The Kingdom of God is not a horizontal plateau where, once we have reached it, there remains no challenge to excel. The Bible speaks of various dimensions and places: His gates, His courts, His presence, the secret place of the most High, etc. In this Kingdom, you can be promoted from a pauper to a prince.

I believe a unique place is reserved for each one who becomes a part of His realm. No one else can occupy that special spot other than the person for whom God has reserved it. It is totally up to each individual to find his privileged position and enter. Jesus bids us to follow, but we decide how far to go.

Everybody Ought to Grow

A friend of mine was building a set of cabinets in his garage. One day his hand slipped off the wood and into the teeth of the table saw, which tore into the flesh around his thumb. Fortunately, he made it to the doctor on time and did not lose any fingers.

The story of his visit to the hospital intrigued me. While stitching up his hand, the doctor told my friend that he had been an atheist in the past. After he became a surgeon who specialized in that particular field, he experienced a complete change of mind. The complexities of the hand, with its intricate nerves and tendons, were so astounding to him that he concluded there had to be a God.

I believe one of the most disabling diseases effecting the Body of Christ is the feeling of insignificance people have because they are not preachers.

Paul compared the Church to a body with many members that each serves a specific purpose. He spoke of the importance of each member, regardless of how insignificant it may appear (see 1 Cor. 12:12-26).

In order for this remarkable Body of Christ to function properly, each member must not only serve in his own rightful capacity, but also recognize the role of others. As Christians we will accomplish our mission, which is to evangelize the world, only by mobilizing every member.

A common feeling among Christians today is that those who occupy pulpits have been elevated to a higher calling than those who make their living by other means. In no way is this correct. Ministers of the gospel are ahead of, not above the saints.

People who have not been selected by God to serve in some facet of the fivefold ministry are not excluded from service to the King. The highest calling is to be a witness for our Lord. Personally, I believe one of the most disabling diseases effecting the Body of Christ is the feeling of insignificance people have because they are not preachers.

We are not under the rule of the Tabernacle of Moses where only the Aaronic priesthood and Levitical order were permitted to minister (see Ex. 28; 38:21; Num. 1:50-53). Rather, we are a part of the prophetic Tabernacle of David where all serve as kings and priests.

Regardless of where we are in our walk with God at the present time, we can advance toward Him and be as close as we choose. There are no limitations barring us from a deeper relationship.

I have never once felt the Holy Spirit give me the cold shoulder while I was in prayer; instead, my experience has proven quite the opposite. Any time I direct my thoughts toward Him or simply whisper His name, Jesus is there.

Gathering from everything I have learned and after being in the presence of God, I have reached the conclusion that He truly enjoys having friends. God does not tire of our company, hoping we will soon leave and not be so persistent in requesting to return.

Friends of God

And the scripture was fulfilled which saith, Abraham believed God, and it was imputed unto him for righteousness: and he was called the Friend of God (James 2:23).

And the Lord spake unto Moses face to face, as a man speaketh unto his friend (Exodus 33:11a).

One of the most valuable commodities a person can have is friends. You may lack in areas where others abound, but if you can number friends among your assets, you are wealthy.

"Friends" is not in the category of things I have enough of. I have several close acquaintances, but I certainly have not filled my quota. I enjoy the challenge of forming new and lasting friendships. For someone to classify me as their friend is an honor I cherish. Elbert Hubbard said, "Your friend is the man who knows all about you and still likes you."[1]

The adage says, "A friend in need is a friend indeed." I value my friends and have found they stand beside me when enemies confront me. I have relied on the support of a comrade's shoulder more than once.

It is my joy in life to find
At every turning of the road
The strong arm of a comrade kind
To help me onward with my load
And since I have no gold to give,
And love alone must make amends
My only prayer is, while I live—
God make me worthy of my friends.[2]

The fierce wrath of an angry God was about to be unleashed on Sodom and Gomorrah as well as on every city of the plain, with the exception of Zoar. The degradation of mankind had plunged far below God's secondary creation, the animal kingdom.

The original transgressions of pride, affluence, lethargy, and negligence had lured them into the vile entrapment of perversion. The putrid odor of the wicked pleasures had nauseated Jehovah.

A God who possesses everlasting mercy was irate with righteous indignation. He was about to reduce this mecca of guiltless indulgence to a heap of ashes.

God is not obligated to consult with a panel of advisors and receive permission to go ahead with His plans. He did, however, reveal His intentions to Abraham.

Abraham encountered a theophany (a pre-incarnate manifestation) of God and voluntarily approached to enter into an arbitration talk on behalf of the people. Abraham admittedly was pushing his friendship with the Lord as he pleaded for mercy. God agreed to Abraham's concession, but 50 righteous could not be found.

Talk continued until Abraham lowered the number of the righteous to ten. Talk about a perfect example of "There goes the neighborhood"! Abraham's voice echoed through the streets, bidding the righteous to come forward, but not even so few as ten responded to him.

History would have recorded the scenario much differently had the Lord had no friend to mediate for the people. Lot and his family escaped the inferno because his uncle had a Friend in high places. (See Genesis 18.)

He made known His ways unto Moses, His acts unto the children of Israel (Psalm 103:7).

Unlike the soldier who obeys orders relayed to him through the chain of command, Moses had access to the war room and deliberated with the Commander in Chief. Moses was not an apprentice assisting a tradesman; he had studied the blueprints and knew the cost and time projections.

Although other prophets received revelation through the subconscious in visions and dreams, Moses enjoyed a dialogue with the Almighty as a friend conversing with a friend.

Moses ascended Mount Sinai and beheld God inscribing tables of stone with His finger. Upon descending the mountain and finding the Israelites participating in idol worship, he dashed the stones in pieces. For the second set, Moses took dictation. (See Exodus 31–34.)

The murmuring and complaining of the Israelites had provoked God into wanting to eradicate them from the face of the earth when Moses stepped into the scene. This unthankful, grumbling bunch was getting to Moses as well. However, he was not about to let Pharaoh have the last laugh. Just like a lawyer approaches the bench, Moses approached God and mediated on behalf of the people.

When the Lord spoke of mercy, Moses grabbed that key word and asked to see His glory. Now, Moses had witnessed a bush on fire that was not consumed. A stick became a snake and vice versa. His hand had instantly become leprous, and just as quickly was cleansed. He saw Egypt inundated with one plague after another while the Israelites in Goshen went unscathed. Then an east wind divided the Red Sea, and Moses and the people witnessed daily the providence of God in the wilderness. Yet, Moses desired to see more.

Miracle-hungry people might possibly be content, but not Moses. He was aware that there was more, and he wanted to see it for himself. His thirst had been quenched, but his hunger was not abated. It was more than a casual request; it was the craving of his soul.

And He said, I will make all My goodness pass before thee, and I will proclaim the name of the Lord before thee; and will be gracious to whom I will be gracious, and will show mercy on whom I will show mercy. And He said, Thou canst not see My face: for there shall no man see Me, and live. And the Lord said, Behold, there is a place by Me, and thou shalt stand upon a rock: and it shall come to pass, while My glory passeth by, that I will put thee in a clift of the rock, and will cover thee with My hand while I pass by (Exodus 33:19-22).

When Moses closed his eyes in death, God not only attended his funeral, He also told the men of Israel to step aside and buried Moses Himself (see Deut. 34:5-6). Many prophets have lived and died, but not one has arisen like Moses.

Abraham and Moses were allowed access to privileged information. They were permitted to enter restricted areas and conduct business with the Almighty.

In this sin-ravaged world destined for the righteous vengeance of an angry God, it is imperative for God to have friends—those who will approach His throne and beg the pardon of those condemned.

The world does not lack for heroes in sports, movies, and music. America is great today because of our heroes from yesterday, the courageous who paid the ultimate price to ensure democracy in this country. The heroes we need today are the kind who can whisper a prayer and change the course of a nation.

The people of the land have used oppression, and exercised robbery, and have vexed the poor and needy: yea, they have oppressed the stranger wrongfully. And I sought for a man among them, that should make up the hedge, and stand in the gap before Me for the land, that I should not destroy it: but I found none. Therefore have I poured out Mine indignation upon them; I have consumed them with the fire of My wrath: their own way have I recompensed upon their heads, saith the Lord God (Ezekiel 22:29-31).

One can see that this subject material is rather important. When we fail to develop a close relationship with God, we rob ourselves as well as others. We are not our own entities; each of us has an obligation to God and our fellow man.

Is there an Esther who will lay her life on the line, petition the king, and spare her people from annihilation? (See Esther 7:1-6.) Are there marked men and women who cry and travail because of the abominations being committed in our cities? Are the priests only in the pulpit? Do they weep between the porch and the altar, saying, "Spare the people of God"? (See Joel 2:17.) Where is the modern-day John Knox who intimidates pompous politicians even more than the fiercest army in the world does?

Failure Is Not Final

David committed adultery with Bathsheba. When he learned that she was pregnant with his child, he conspired to have her husband killed (see 2 Sam. 11). Living under the rule of a king who participated in this type of immoral behavior would not have been easy.

David did not have to hire a string of attorneys to represent him before Congress to save him from impeachment. He did, however, have to pay his dues to God.

After repenting and suffering the consequences for the crime, David still merited a status given to no other: He is the only one in the Bible called *a man after God's own heart* (see 1 Sam. 13:14; Acts 13:22).

Where is the modern-day John Knox who intimidates pompous politicians even more than the fiercest army in the world does?

An adulterer who committed cold-blooded murder is not restricted from advancing in the Kingdom? That is the unparalleled beauty of contrition and repentance. When we mess up, we can get up if we refuse to give up.

Our pasts cannot stop us. Excuses will not exonerate us; nor can satan keep us from finding our place in the Kingdom. The ball lies in our court. Whether we will pursue our post or be pacified with the present is up to us.

God did not give up on David because David would not let go of God. He harnessed his desires and lusts and channeled them toward Heaven. Herein lay the secret of David's restoration.

As the hart panteth after the water brooks, so panteth my soul after Thee, O God (Psalm 42:1).

Being Least Isn't Bad

John the Baptist was called the forerunner of Christ. It is quite obvious from the Scriptures that John did not purchase his wardrobe from any of the high-end clothiers. He lacked social graces, and his diet did not impress me in any way.

However, when he spoke, people listened. John drew a larger crowd in the desert than we can attract to our modern, air-conditioned edifices. They did not come for the music or a program; they attended his crude, arid, uncomfortable services and listened to fearless, sin-rebuking preaching because he was a man sent from God (see Mt. 3:1-12).

One would think this was the ultimate, that John the Baptist had to be the greatest. Not so. God has a place reserved for us in the Kingdom that exceeds John's. He was born *with* the Spirit; you and I are born *of* the Spirit.

I do not deem myself worthy to be in the same room with John the Baptist. Nonetheless, according to the Scriptures, if I hold the title as being the least in the Kingdom of God, then I have excelled beyond John. If this is the least I can be, than I am in awe when I think of what more I can be.

> *Verily I say unto you, Among them that are born of women there hath not risen a greater than John the Baptist: notwithstanding he that is least in the kingdom of heaven is greater than he* (Matthew 11:11).

Pay careful attention as we examine the people who surrounded our Lord, for you will find yourself in one of these categories. The good news is, if you are not pleased with where you find yourself, you can change to another any time you choose.

Investments With No Return

The 5,000 whom Jesus fed with five loaves of bread and two fishes enjoyed the miracles. They were attracted to the spectacular. As long as Jesus was ministering to their needs and not to their souls, they stayed around.

When Jesus began to talk about the Kingdom of God and the cost of discipleship, one by one they began to leave. When it came to giving rather than getting, feeding rather than feasting, and dying rather than dining, they left. (See John 6.)

This category of people requires a lot of maintenance but has very little impact. The place in the Kingdom where they have arrived tastes good and feels good as long as self-denial is not mentioned. They are comfortable as long as they are being ministered to, but they faint away when asked to minister. To them, *sacrifice* is an ancient word that ended at Calvary.

Committing time, money, and effort to a local church will not happen. They constantly run from place to place, following the latest trend. Rather than develop a personal prayer life and ingest the Bible, they flock to prophets as if they were gurus.

Whenever mountains—intended to build character and increase faith—are in their pathway, they choose an alternate route. They want smooth highways and ideal weather. The multitudes were always sent away whenever challenging situations arose. They were not compatible with storms and cries.

Their perspective of God remains one-dimensional. They leave with their bellies full of fish, thinking that is the ultimate, while robbing themselves of greater revelation of the deity of Christ. They seemingly are not aware of the fact that while their natural man is fed, their spiritual man is starving.

Our Lord multiplied the bread and fish lest they should faint on their way home. They were in a desert place and needed sustenance. Christ demonstrated great concern for their physical well-being in providing food for them.

I have personally experienced healing in my body on several occasions. I have witnessed the Lord provide financially for my

> *The question is, do you want to be a depository or a disciple? a conductor or a container?*

family too many times to mention. The Lord desires that we lean on Him and look to Him when in need.

In no way do I want to trivialize the necessities of the natural man. Fish and bread are important. However, the 5,000 stunted their spiritual growth by leaving when they should have stayed. The next dimension of ministry by our Lord was intended to put meat on the bones of their spirit man.

The question is, do you want to be a depository or a disciple? a conductor or a container? Are you content to live at the base camp or will you embark on the climb to see things from a higher perspective? Are you content with observing Christ through the lens of a telescope when you can come close and scrutinize every inch of Him under a microscope?

Supernatural, Not Spectacular

Jesus commissioned the 70 to go in groups of two and minister salvation, healing, and deliverance. Their assignment was almost identical to that of the 12 disciples. I am an advocate of ministering in the Spirit, and I am saddened over the lack of the supernatural demonstration of the Holy Spirit in most churches today.

There is not a shortage of God's power, but rather of prayer and fasting to move into this realm of spiritual authority. I understand that we all have our calling; however, the local church should have these gifts in operation.

We are not justified in simply having an open mind to the gifts. The Bible admonishes us to earnestly covet them (see 1 Cor. 12:31). Let me offer a little advice. If you are a layperson and feel that God desires to use you in this area, I recommend that you seek the counsel of your pastor. (I do not, in any way, want to cause strife in a congregation.)

If your pastor makes provision for the operation of the gifts of the Spirit, then work with him, under the covering of his leadership.

Remember, laity is not the authority of the local assembly. A wise man once said, "Authority without accountability breeds anarchy." Great moves of God have been aborted by people who were used of God but who refused to submit to authority.

If the pastor does not believe that these gifts are for today, then find another place of worship so as to not cause division and strife. Do not take it upon yourself to try to alter the course of the congregation.

The gifts of the Spirit have received a lot of bad press due to less-than-real individuals operating them. This should not be a reason for us to be robbed of the genuine move of the Spirit. There always will be phonies and those with ulterior motives in every walk of life.

And the seventy returned again with joy, saying, Lord, even the devils are subject unto us through Thy name. And He said unto them, I beheld Satan as lightning fall from heaven. Behold, I give unto you power to tread on serpents and scorpions, and over all the power of the enemy: and nothing shall by any means hurt you. Notwithstanding in this rejoice not, that the spirits are subject unto you; but rather rejoice, because your names are written in heaven (Luke 10:17-20).

This is the only negative I see concerning the 70. They were like children playing with toys; they did not understand the purpose of power.

As important as it is to place emphasis on the supernatural, it is also necessary to realize that demonstration without dedication is dangerous. I am not implying that the 70 were transgressors; I am saying that it is possible to be used by God and not be devoted to Him.

Possessing power and not purity is like being a vigilante with a dangerous weapon. Eventually someone is going to be fatally wounded. There are far too many casualties caused by those who operated in the gifts but who did not manifest any fruit of the Spirit.

If we see only the hand of God and fail to seek the heart of God, we will be susceptible to repeating the same mistake the 70 made.

Two words that cannot be overemphasized on this topic are *motive* and *purpose*.

> *Many will say to Me in that day, Lord, Lord, have we not prophesied in Thy name? and in Thy name have cast out devils? and in Thy name done many wonderful works? And then will I profess unto them, I never knew you: depart from Me, ye that work iniquity* (Matthew 7:22-23).

The word *knew* in this passage comes from the Greek word *ginosko*, which means allow, be aware, feel, perceive, can speak, be sure, understand.[3] The Lord is saying, "Leave! I am not aware of you, I don't perceive who you are, and I can't be sure of you."

We must take every precaution necessary to avoid becoming infatuated with power. It is essential that we understand the objective of the anointing, which is to destroy yokes holding people captive (see Is. 10:27).

To know God is to know power, but to know power does not mean you know God.

To know God is to know power, but to know power does not mean you know God. A sure way to guard oneself against erring in this area is to follow Paul's teachings in First Corinthians 13. When compassion for the needs of others becomes our motive, we are safeguarded from failure.

Charisma Without Character

The distinction I notice between the 70 and the 12 disciples is fellowship with the Lord. The disciples also were given power over sickness and demonic influences, but it appears they experienced a more intimate relationship with Jesus.

Unlike the 70, the disciples beheld Him performing His first miracle, walking on water, and sleeping in storms, and they dipped their bread with Him at His final passion.

Jesus knowing that the Father had given all things into His hands, and that He was come from God, and went to God; He riseth from supper, and laid aside His garments; and took a towel, and girded Himself. After that He poureth water into a basin, and began to wash the disciples' feet, and to wipe them with the towel wherewith He was girded (John 13:3-5).

The King of kings washed the dusty feet of His disciples, demonstrating His willing service to humanity. The Master's hands on our head result in healing; His hands on our feet result in humility.

Rather than being wooed by power, the 12 disciples received instruction on the true definition of ministry. The secret to avoiding arrogance and evolving into pretentious hierarchy is to always be willing to serve.

In 1983, Dan Rigdon, the pastor I am honored to work with, traveled to Calcutta, India. He thought how wonderful it would be to visit Mother Teresa, but he considered such a meeting to be next to impossible. With her extremely busy itinerary, she could be anywhere in the world. Even if she was in Calcutta, taking time with him did not seem probable. Nevertheless, he called Mother Teresa's residence. To his great surprise, not only was she home, but she also consented to see him.

As Pastor Rigdon sat with Mother Teresa, he asked her as to how she entered this type of ministry. She explained that as a young girl she asked God how to continually be in His presence without ever leaving. Mother Teresa said the Lord impressed the following Scriptures upon her; by obeying them, she was ever in the presence of the Lord.

For I was an hungered, and ye gave Me meat: I was thirsty, and ye gave Me drink: I was a stranger, and ye took Me in: naked, and ye clothed Me: I was sick, and ye visited Me: I was in prison, and ye came unto Me (Matthew 25:35-36).

Mother Teresa associated herself with the poorest of the poor. This little lady, who barely stood five feet tall, was content to wear a sari rather than the latest fashion statement. She conversed with world leaders only on behalf of the poor and not for personal recognition.

As Pastor Rigdon listened intently to Mother Teresa, he noticed nuns in the next room having devotions. Although he could not speak the Indian dialect, he recognized the song they were singing.

To be like Jesus, to be like Jesus,
On earth I long to be like Him.
All through life's journey
From earth to glory
I only ask to be like Him.[4]

Some of the nuns laid prostrate on the floor while others stood with hands raised. It was obvious that they were echoing the sentiments of the lady who epitomized compassion for those who were victims of poverty and misfortune.

Beholding someone ministering in the supernatural with a servant's heart rather than as a pompous playboy soliciting acclamation is a beautiful thing.

Charisma without character breeds cynicism. People's confidence in the ministry is submerged in a sea of disillusionment after they hear shocking revelations of secret lives and ungodly activity.

The operation of the gifts of the Spirit are accentuated by the manifestation of the fruit of the Spirit. Beholding someone ministering in the supernatural with a servant's heart rather than as a pompous playboy soliciting acclamation is a beautiful thing.

Partial But Not Prejudiced

The numbers dissipate rapidly as we continue our study of those who pursued a deeper relationship with Christ. We no longer find ourselves shoulder to shoulder amid thousands, but among a handful.

There are ample Scriptures that support the fact that Christ was partial, but certainly not prejudiced toward anyone. When He went to Jairus' house to resurrect his daughter, He permitted only Peter, James, and John to go with Him (see Mk. 5:35-37). When our Lord was transfigured and stood alongside Moses and Elijah, once again He invited only Peter, James, and John to go with Him (see Mt. 17:1-4).

Those two examples substantiate the fact that Jesus showed partiality. However, the fact that Judas, who betrayed Him, was part of His group of disciples and that Peter, who denied Him, was a member of the inner circle shows His lack of prejudice.

Judas Iscariot was a devilish man who betrayed his dearest friend, delivering Jesus to the enemy. Yet, he was not ousted from the brotherhood. Peter denied three times that he ever met the Master, but even knowing this in advance, Christ granted Peter access to be one of those closest to Him.

I reiterate: Christ delights in having friends. He does not require perfection, but He will not condone our sin. He is willing to take the risk of letting us enjoy His companionship, hoping we will forsake iniquity and cling solely to Him.

Why were Peter, James, and John permitted to go when their contemporaries were not invited? The answer is quite simple. Their ambition to be with Christ afforded them perks and privileges.

The Lord does not reward our status, but our diligence. Actually, we choose the amount of time we spend with the Lord. Do we want a quick fix, or do we desire to revel in His presence, leaving edified and revitalized?

How Close Can One Get?

Now there was leaning on Jesus' bosom one of His disciples, whom Jesus loved. Simon Peter therefore beckoned to him, that he should ask who it should be of whom He spake.

17

The Impassioned Soul

He then lying on Jesus' breast saith unto Him, Lord, who is it? (John 13:23-25)

The atmosphere in the room was heavy with emotion. Hardy, masculine disciples openly displayed their feelings regarding the future of their leader. Several were questioning, one was leaving, and the beloved disciple was listening to Heaven's heartbeat. The 12 disciples were chosen by Jesus; the inner circle chose Jesus. The beloved disciple clung to Jesus. The die was cast; the precedent was established; we can come as close to Christ as we desire.

The place of solitude with the Lord is a chamber, not a conference room. The carpet does not indicate significant wear; one will not have to elbow his way through crowded corridors to get there. Expansion plans would be wonderful, if they were necessary. Presently there appears to be ample space.

This is not an amusement park for juvenile Christians to participate in frivolity. It is not a banquet hall with exquisite entrees and exceptional ambiance.

Our Lord mentioned entering a closet to pray (see Mt. 6:6). Personally, I have never seen a closet that could accommodate a lot of people. He is not referring to a literal closet, but to a place where the two of you can meet.

Not many can cite the exact address of this locale. They are able to point you in the general direction, but having never ventured there themselves, they are not familiar with the floor plan.

This is not an amusement park for juvenile Christians to participate in frivolity. It is not a banquet hall with exquisite entrees and exceptional ambiance. It is a holy convocation attended only by a few; it is not a camp meeting packed with thousands.

Those who enter have paid their dues and are there to conduct important business. They have not stumbled on this secret place accidentally; they have been on their knees and in the Book searching for clues.

Like hostage negotiators, they stand between two totally opposite worlds, vying for the souls of lost humanity. Decisions will be made there that will endure throughout eternity.

These people are pacesetters, not jetsetters; they are world changers, not miracle chasers. Mingling in crowds is not their forte, but quality time with Christ is their priority. They eat the loaves and fishes, but they exist on the Bread of Life (see Jn. 6:35).

It is a holy convocation attended only by a few; it is not a camp meeting packed with thousands.

When they first caught a glimpse of Him, it was love at first sight. Ever since then, they passionately pursued to win the heart of God. Though some experience success in business and enjoy affluent lifestyles, relationship with Christ is paramount.

Church, to them, does not commence Sunday morning and conclude Sunday evening. Their homes are sanctuaries of praise and the workplace their field of labor. Although prayer can be exhausting, they are on call 24 hours a day, ready to volunteer for whatever emergency that arises.

I do not believe I can overemphasize the importance of intercessors. This generation *must* possess selfless individuals who loathe mediocrity and continually hunger for revival.

Those who choose this path walk a lonely road, many times being misunderstood. What others fail to understand is that by separating from complaining carnality, these people have stood in the cleft of the rock and beheld the glory of God.

Endnotes

1. As quoted in Dorothy Carnegie, ed., *Dale Carnegie's Scrapbook: A Treasury of the Wisdom of the Ages* (New York: Simon and Schuster, 1959), 164.

2. Frank Dempster Sherman, "Lyrics of Joy," as quoted in Carnegie, ed., *Dale Carnegie's Scrapbook*, 65.

3. James Strong, *Strong's Exhaustive Concordance of the Bible* (Nashville, TN: Crusade Bible Publishers, Inc., n.d.), # 1097.

4. L.R. Ooton, "To Be Like Him." Sing Unto the Lord © 1978 (Hazelwood, MO: Word Aflame Press), 347.

Chapter Two

Passion

One thing have I desired of the Lord, that will I seek after;
that I may dwell in the house of the Lord all the days of my life,
to behold the beauty of the Lord, and to inquire in His temple.
Psalm 27:4

No Christ, No Life

"On a hill far away stands an old rugged cross...." Hours before, a bloodthirsty mob witnessed the execution of an innocent man. Although multiplied millions of people have fallen to the ground in battle, by accident, by execution, or by murder, no other death has had the effect as this heinous event.

The earth shook and trembled. The sun blanketed her face. A robust Roman soldier commissioned to the crucifixion struck his chest with the palm of his hand, realizing the identity of the condemned (see Mt. 27:35-54).

Sin's ransom had been paid. Never again would the blood of an animal be shed to atone for the transgressions of humanity. As Jesus ventured into the jaws of death, others already in its dreadful grasp made their exit.

As you gazed at the hillside, a crevice caused by an earthquake caught your attention, along with patches of grass stained with blood. Then the faint sound of sobbing reached your ears. Searching the hill with your eyes, you saw the silhouette of someone kneeling in footprints imbedded in the soil by the sandals of the executioners.

The "place of the skull" is vacated—with the exception of one despondent soul in whom the crucifixion produced a void so deep that it erased any reason to go on living.

The last person to pull herself away from Calvary was Mary Magdalene. How could there be any life without Christ? She had lived a good portion of her life never knowing true love, only to have it walk up to her and call her by name. It was an encounter never to be forgotten.

The men in her past had been interested in one thing: how Mary could please them. This Man was different. He did not offer a piece of silver for a moment of pleasure. He did not gaze at her with leering eyes, but with warmth and compassion.

The tormenting demons that had dominated her mind and vexed her spirit were set at bay at His command. The empty, aching heart stained with sin was cleansed. A conscience that had slumped her shoulders and pulled her chin to the ground was relieved of condemnation.

Mary's relationship with this Galilean was of the purest form. Self-respect and identity were restored. From that point on she sought to please only Jesus. Never again would she stoop to satisfy the lusts of men.

When Christ becomes your life, there can be no life without Him. The encounter between a woman of the night and the Savior of the world left her never the same. Mary Magdalene was forever indebted to this Man. Her passion in life was to be near Him. If there is no Christ, where will she go?

Feeling only emptiness and not daring to consider tomorrow, Mary slowly descended the hillside. Waking up with no Christ is as impractical as a day with no sun. There can be no such thing. So it is with not having Jesus.

Love's melody was silenced. Mary's new life had suffered a fatal wound. It was good while it lasted, but it was evidently too good to be true. Still, she would never forget this magnificent Christ. As an epitaph is chiseled in granite, He was forever etched in her mind. Was it possible to survive on memories?

The miracle of salvation made such an impact on my family that it brought about a complete transformation. The Christ who had been on the peripheral was relocated to the center of our lives.

The dad shackled by alcohol was gloriously liberated; his desire for the world was turned to a thirst after the Spirit. A brokenhearted mother who had endured much grief in life witnessed the salvaging and restoration of her home. Sons and daughters born into a dysfunctional family were re-born into the Kingdom of God. The coffee table, once cluttered with beer bottles, now held the family Bible. Praise replaced profanity. Prayer meetings replaced drinking binges. Some of my siblings were gloriously filled with the Holy Spirit in the same house where there used to be fighting and discord.

Christ became our life. The portable phonograph in our living room was constantly playing gospel records. Whenever neighbors would stop by to visit, at some point the conversation focused on the goodness of God.

We crammed into the car to attend camp meetings, conferences, and fellowship services. When the opportunity presented itself, my dad would stand and testify of the grace of God. His speech hinted not of excellence, but of experience.

To us his voice was more agonizing than angelic as he sat beside the old oil stove singing his favorite hymn *The Last Mile of the Way*.

However, in Heaven even the angels listened intently as my dad struggled to stay in tune as he sang of finishing life's race.

In November of 1970 our large family squeezed into the first few rows of pews in the little Pentecostal church we attended to bid farewell to Father. Although he had been a failure in the first several laps of his race, he crossed the finish line in victory.

I vividly remember my mother's words as she testified with her soft-spoken voice: "I thank the Lord for saving my soul. I have no reason to turn back and no hard-luck story to tell."

This dear woman exemplified passion. I remember times as I was growing up when we did not own an automobile. Often the temperature would fall far below freezing. These would appear to be legitimate excuses for staying home, but Mother would bundle us up and we would set out for church, whether it was for Sunday night service or Tuesday night Bible study.

I especially remember the time Mother received the news that her house had burned to the ground. Stay home from church? No way. She collected herself, went off to church, and gave her hallmark testimony. Losing the homestead and not having sufficient means to replace it was no justification for ill feelings toward God.

Today Mother is no longer with us. Our family was blessed beyond words to still have her after she came close to death's door on several occasions. She was the glue that keeps this enormous family from becoming disconnected.

Although at times she became confused due to setbacks brought on by illness, Mother was faithful to prayer. She might have become disoriented about where she lives, but she never thought of crawling into bed before kneeling in prayer.

Once when I visited with her, I was honored to kneel with her at her bedside and go through the list of names on her prayer list. That list was written on tablets in her heart, though, not on a piece of paper. She had spoken the names so frequently to the Lord that she needed no "cheat sheet" to remind her.

Mother understood that life was slowing down for her. She got terribly frustrated over the restrictions forced onto her because of poor health. Somehow she managed to get through each day. She had the will to survive with the loss of health, but she never would entertain thoughts of life without Christ.

To some He is like a balm for their conscience. To the Marys, He is as essential as the air they breathe.

If at all possible, she still attended church, singing, and claping her hands in the familiar style she developed through the years. Even with her health problems, she attended a prayer meeting and was on her knees every bit of 45 minutes.

Many find it too difficult to live for Him. The true Christian cannot live without Him. To some He is like a balm for their conscience. To the Marys, He is as essential as the air they breathe.

What do you see when you picture Christ? Many see Him as a healer. And He is; He is Jehovah-Rapha. Others see Him as the cure for their financial woes. And He is; He is Jehovah-Jireh. But Mary sees Him as life personified. To her, He is everything.

Having a personal relationship with Jesus Christ goes beyond church membership. You must have an insatiable desire that does not permit you to boycott spending time with Him. Anything short of intimacy simply will not cut it for you.

The Ark of the Covenant, which represented the presence of God, was to be situated in the center of the camp of Israel (see Num. 2:17; 4; 10; 1 Chron. 16:1). God intended to be involved with every aspect of Israel's life. It may be time for you to bring Christ from the perimeter and place Him in the vortex—the very center—of your life.

Seeking Christ

Sunday morning, before the sun had risen, Mary was up. The weekend had seemed to be unusually long. It had been days since she saw the Lover of her soul. Her aching heart could wait no longer to be near Him. The last to leave Calvary was the first to arrive at the tomb. She did not come expecting a resurrected body, however; she was there to anoint a corpse.

To Mary's dismay, the grave was empty. In the past men had used her and then left her, leaving her heart wrenching in destitution. Mary had never felt more alone than when Jesus lowered His head and died. Now an empty tomb plunged her into a depth of loneliness she had never before experienced.

Panic-stricken, Mary ran and found Peter and "the other disciple, whom Jesus loved," and announced, "They have taken away the Lord out of the sepulchre, and we know not where they have laid Him" (Jn. 20:2). As the two disciples sprinted toward the tomb, the "other disciple" arrived first. Stooping down, he peeked inside and noticed the grave clothes.

The "other disciple" then followed Peter into the tomb and became an instant believer. However, their minds were troubled at the placement of the grave clothes. Puzzled by the missing body, they returned to their homes. But not Mary. She remained at the entrance of the tomb weeping. What was there to go home to? How could life possibly go on with no Christ? (See John 20.)

There was no way she could return to any kind of normalcy in her life without Him. Her life was interrupted and could not resume until she was sure of where her Lord was.

Extravagant Praise

Some writers suggest that Mary Magdalene was simpleminded. Potential might not have been part of her portfolio, but passion was. With her heart panting to see her Lord, she could think of nothing else to do and nowhere else to go.

Mary was the type of person who could not pass by without expressing gratitude to the One responsible for the peace in her life.

Simon the Pharisee did not exercise even common courtesy by washing the feet of Christ (see Lk. 7:36-46). One saw Him as the mender of broken furniture; the other saw Him as the mender of broken hearts.

Mary would never think of getting by on just what was expected. She anointed Him with an ointment so costly and precious that the robe and tunic of the Lord carried the scent of sacrificial praise (see Lk. 7:38).

In the future someone would cast a lot, acquire the robe of Jesus, and encounter the redolence of unselfish giving (see Jn. 19:23-24). What a treasure! Rather than take away from its value, those stains added to the garment's worth—a cloth smelling of perfume and soiled with blood from the Lamb of God.

Mary's past life of ill repute had emitted a horrendous odor. Then the atmosphere was permeated with the pleasant incense of a life set free. The sweet fragrance of exorbitant adulation filtered through the house that reeked with the pungency of self-righteousness. Some viewed it as a terrible waste; the perfume was worth a year's wages (see Mk. 14:5; Jn. 12:5). But praise to the One responsible for handing your life back to you is never too extravagant.

Mary had no need of water from an outside source. Internal rivers of living water provided plenty. Passion sprang from her heart, producing tears that streamed down her face. His feet were soaked from the distillation of her soul. Weeping, she knelt and dried the Master's feet with her glory (see Lk. 7:38; 1 Cor. 11:15).

Had Mary reverted to her old ways of exhibiting flirtatious conduct? A thousand times no! She had *entered the gates of worship*. In this dimension of intimate supplication, formality is forbidden.

Had it been a celebrity, politician, or any manner of famous person, protocol would have been sufficient. Some have earned respect; Jesus merits praise.

Simon the Pharisee's objective was to impress Christ by inviting Him into his house. Mary's mind-set was the exact opposite. To stand in His presence and render thanks exceeded her ultimate aspirations.

Today we are inhibited by a lack of desire rather than a lack of time. Distractions that bid for our attention prevail over spending time with our Lord. Self-gratification conquers servanthood. An old cliché says that "we get through praying but don't pray through." When passion returns to our hearts, power will return to our gatherings.

Smith Wigglesworth, the turn-of-the-century apostle of faith, said, "Sometimes I don't pray more than thirty minutes. But I don't go more than thirty minutes without praying." In his book, *Power Through Prayer*, E.M. Bounds wrote about Edward Payson, who wore grooves into the hardwood boards where his knees pressed so often and so long as he knelt in prayer.[1]

The Full Gospel Church in Saint John, New Brunswick, Canada, experienced a sovereign move of God in the mid-1950's. The pastors, known simply as the Davis Sisters, spent their entire mornings in prayer. If someone happened to ring the doorbell at that time of day, the visitor was told, "We will be in prayer throughout the morning; you are welcome to join us. If not, you will have to return later."

The Pentecostals of Alexandria, Louisiana, began a 24-hour prayer chain in the early 1970's that remains unbroken to this day. The prayer shifts are three hours each. This church is located in a city of approximately 50,000 people. Although their membership has been greatly affected due to economic setbacks, they have 2,500 people in regular attendance, and they are growing rapidly.

The fine leadership of this church has established in the hearts of their parishioners a relentless pursuit of revival. At any given moment the sound of intercessory prayer echoes through the corridors of the sanctuary.

We do a terrible injustice to our children if we neglect to seek the face of God. Contemporary music accounts for the biggest percentage of what they hear in our churches. It is imperative that they hear the cries of God's people as they travail over the fallen state of humanity.

Passion is that magnetic force of energy that has the ability to push and pull. It is the power necessary to boost us from the launching pad and into orbit, in spite of being inept. It is the winch that pulls us from the pit of despair.

Recorded in the pages of history are innumerable examples of those challenged by a lack of ability, yet who succeeded because of passion. Something inside them refused to surrender to limitations. When intellect, physical strength, or natural ability were not in abundance, they fell back on that burning desire to achieve.

Mary was on a mission. She refused to vacate the tomb without knowing where her Savior was. Emptiness from her past threatened to return. She could not allow the chasm—filled only by Christ—to reopen and swallow her. *Where was the Lord?*

Passion is that magnetic force that has the ability to push and pull. It is the power necessary to boost us from the launching pad and into orbit, in spite of being inept.

Within the child of God burns a yearning so intense it causes him to pray without ceasing. It removes him from the supper table and draws him into the prayer closet. In the midst of a crowd, it can make him feel alone.

We labor long hours and take on extra jobs to purchase material possessions that fail to pacify the inner cry of the soul. We study the globe and plan our next vacation, only to return weary. We munch on antacid tablets to soothe inflamed ulcers as we fret over tomorrow, hoping our nest egg will be enough.

There is a place, a Utopia, that does not require arduous flights over oceans. Cares of this world are not permitted beyond its walls. Whether the Dow Jones is making history with gains or plunging into unprecedented losses is of no concern here. Should Wall Street collapse, these walls will remain intact.

There is a haven whose tranquil shores offer shelter from life's angry waves. The Master's arms are ever open to embrace the storm-tossed sailor and rescue him from his sinking vessel.

Thou wilt show me the path of life: in Thy presence is fulness of joy; at Thy right hand there are pleasures for evermore (Psalm 16:11).

Undivided Attention

Two angels in shining garments appeared before Mary and asked her why she wept (see Jn. 20:12-13). Notice that neither her weeping nor her search ended with the arrival of angels. Her reply came from a heart whose longing could be satisfied only with the body of Christ, whether dead or alive.

Because they have taken away my Lord, and I know not where they have laid Him (John 20:13b).

Others might have been captivated by these two, perhaps tall, handsome celestial beings in brilliant robes. Not Mary. Her attention was focused solely on Jesus. Even in the company of angels she was not distracted from her purpose in being there. Her passion kept her lingering at Calvary, induced sleep deprivation, and pulled her from bed early that morning.

I am elated over the news of churches receiving great outpourings of the Holy Spirit. Man-made barriers are collapsing as the Spirit crosses into denominational lines.

Tenets and traditions will restrain the hungry no longer. "East is east and west is west and never the twain shall meet" is no longer a truism. The wall that Churchill called "the Iron Curtain" separated countrymen and divided families for decades. Ronald Reagan ignited a flame that burned on both sides when he defied socialism and challenged Mikhail Gorbachev to tear down the Berlin Wall.

Years of division and dictatorship came to an abrupt end as young men and women, refusing to exist in an evil empire, climbed on top of the cement structure. With whatever tools they could get their hands on, they chipped away inch by inch until they removed the barricade that had kept them oppressed and apart.

The world is experiencing what is quite possibly the greatest move of God ever known to man. The birthing room for this Heaven-sent, hell-shaking, life-changing experience is the prayer room.

An appetite that demands holiness unto the Lord has gripped the hearts of God's people. Social acceptance, approval from peers, and all other carnal ambitions are losing in this day of spiritual awakening.

Social acceptance, approval from peers, and all other carnal ambitions are losing in this day of spiritual awakening.

In this time of spiritual renewal, we will experience miraculous healings and divine visitations. There is no such thing as a day of miracles, but there is a God of miracles, and He remains the same. Once again cities infiltrated by gangs will be turned upside down as disillusioned youth lay down weapons and take up crosses.

Amid this great Holy Ghost demonstration, we as the Church must keep our eyes steadfast on Jesus. Healings and divine visitations are God-given manifestations for the purpose of enhancing our desire to know Him. Heaven is to be our home; Christ is to be our quest.

Every song we sing, every sermon we preach, and each time we meet should be with the intent of exalting Christ. We should never be found guilty of preaching the name of our organizations and denominations, but rather the name of Jesus alone. Only His name is worthy of praise and capable of salvation.

Our doctrines and edifices should not be the objects of our worship. We dare not make idols of the vessels God uses to demonstrate His power. His holy eminence, the Lord Jesus Christ, must be the center of our praise.

The Holy Spirit must have preeminence in our lives. We must not dull the sword of the Spirit by dictating what can and cannot be preached by God's ministers. Like a cancer left unattended, any malignant tumors that inhabit our spirits will lead to our demises. We may feel temporary discomfort as God extracts the problem. But the Word of the Lord in the skilled hands of the Surgeon will produce a healthy soul drawn much closer to God.

The Hungry Shall Be Filled

As Mary Magdalene turned away from the angels, a man she perceived to be the gardener spoke to her. This supposed stranger asked her the same question:

Woman, why weepest thou? whom seekest thou? (John 20:15a)

"Why am I weeping and seeking? The answer is simple. It is for my Lord." Her anxiety blinded her. The One she sought was talking with her. Never once thinking that her passion would warrant her an audience with a resurrected Savior, Mary continued to try and locate His body.

She, supposing Him to be the gardener, saith unto Him, Sir, if Thou have borne Him hence, tell me where Thou hast laid Him, and I will take Him away (John 20:15b).

Mary addressed the One she was passionately looking for as *Him*. She took it for granted that this stranger would know who *He* is. When Jesus strolled into Mary's life, He took center stage. In her world there is only one *Him*.

The question she posed may be proof of her being simpleminded. "If You have taken Him, tell me where He is and I will take Him away." We have no clue as to the stature or physical strength Mary possessed. We do know that she was a woman. Putting everything into perspective, it is not reasonable that she could negotiate the corpse of Christ on her own.

Mary was thinking with love rather than logic. The affection she had for Him caused her to overlook natural circumstances. If the body of Christ was randomly stowed or misplaced, she would make sure it rested in peace.

You came to Christ and witnessed a metamorphosis in your life. Not only did others notice a significant change, but you yourself were astonished at what transpired. A new zeal prompted you to proclaim that you would convert the world to Christ, if need be, on your own.

The experience of salvation was so effective that it intoxicated your heart and erased rationality. Every thought that entered your mind was of Him. Eventually we all come to realize that just our own efforts are not adequate to evangelize this world.

If we could only recapture the fervent passion that does not acknowledge limitations! The inertia that impedes revival is no match for this infinite fervor.

Unsolicited praise will replace begging for a response. Church attendance records will be broken, forcing us into building programs to facilitate the masses. Missions giving will increase drastically, making it possible for our missionaries to return to their respected fields of labor instead of traversing across the nation wearing out vehicles and themselves, pleading for funds.

Gone is the day of intimidating people into volunteering their time and efforts to the church. We are not going to participate just because it is the right thing to do. Frustrated pastors and burned-out evangelists are capitulating to this lethargic attitude much too frequently. Our mission statement remains the same, but it has a greater demand. We must win the lost at any cost.

In Singapore the government conducts random backyard inspections for standing water. The residence that is discovered having such a pool is served with a fine. Why? Mosquitoes breed in stagnant water.

Churches that lack missionary zeal and have lost the vision of a dying world become a breeding ground for a plethora of spiritual bacteria and germs. There is no flow of the Spirit in or out.

These institutions of complacency with the "us four and no more" attitude eventually die due to lack of new life. The members doze off in the comfort zone, failing to awaken in time to be saved from extinction. Although there is an abundance of indoor fighting, there is an immense deficit of a burden for the unsaved.

The hope for billions of people en route to a Godless eternity is for the Church to be engulfed in a flame of passion. Vacant prayer closets must be revisited and not abandoned until Heaven has issued a statement.

Jesus saith unto her, Mary. She turned herself, and saith unto Him, Rabboni; which is to say, Master (John 20:16).

Think back to the time when God called your name. You might not have heard an audible voice, but you undoubtedly knew that He was speaking to you. Your moment in time had arrived. The Almighty singled you out, and the gravity of His unfathomable love lured you to Him.

Vacant prayer closets must be revisited and not abandoned until Heaven has issued a statement.

You accepted an invitation and attended church. It was a totally different environment from what you were used to. Thoughts of rejection were quickly dismissed by the warm smiles of the friendliest people you had ever encountered.

From the opening prayer and throughout the time of worship, something kept tugging at your heartstrings. From the moment the preacher read his text to the altar call at the end, you were convinced someone gave him the scoop on you. When he looked out over the audience, his eyes seemed to be fastened directly on you.

You sank to your knees and lifted your hands, and you became the recipient of a second chance.

You felt as if it were just you and God alone in the universe. Overcome with conviction, you made your way slowly down the aisle. Your flesh screamed at you to turn back, but you kept on walking. Imps of darkness taunted your mind, telling you that you could never live this kind of life. Yet you sank to your knees and lifted your hands, and you became the recipient of a second chance.

There were occasions along the way when you staggered and maybe even stumbled, but you kept on walking. Unlike driving on interstate highways with ample lanes and smooth blacktop, you negotiated turns and accelerated for hills while dodging potholes. Your journey originated when Christ spoke your name; it will conclude just the same way.

Jesus could allow Mary's lonesome heart to ache no longer. Early on Sunday morning in a cemetery still damp with dew, the morbid quietness was broken. The eerie, empty burial chamber was eclipsed by the risen Son. Like the wake from a pebble tossed into a pond, the compassionate sound of "Mary" interrupted the silence.

The distinction in His voice went undetected as Jesus asked Mary the reason for her weeping. But when He called her by name, there was no mistaking who was talking. "Master," replied Mary. No longer a servant to sin, she was a love slave to Christ (see Jn. 20:16).

With all probability, in times past Mary had been addressed by a myriad of titles, most of which would make an unconscionable sailor blush. Now Christ beckoned to her by name, reminding Mary of her present status, not her past sins.

The Entrance Key

Jesus saith unto her, Touch Me not; for I am not yet ascended to My Father (John 20:17a).

Between hell and Heaven, Jesus made a stopover. Upon ascending from the regions of the damned en route to be glorified, something came up. An appointment with His Father is of utmost importance, but a simpleminded woman weeping at His tomb merited priority. Mary beheld the risen Christ before anyone else did. "You can look, but you can't touch," He said.

The Impassioned Soul

At an earlier date, while on His way to Jairus' house to heal his daughter, Christ was delayed. A penniless woman with an affliction that physicians could not cure forged through a crowd and, with desperate hands, touched the hem of His robe (see Lk. 8:41-56). In each incident, timing was precise. The woman arose and the daughter awoke. Both were made whole.

Before Jesus entered the room without using the door to meet with His disciples, He chatted with Mary. She did not have membership into the ecclesiastical alliance, and she certainly was not compatible for the Mensa society. In spite of her lack of status, she gained access to Christ even before the beloved disciple.

David repenting...Hannah whispering...Rachel pleading...Jacob wrestling (see Ps. 51:2; 1 Sam. 1:13; Gen. 30:1; 32:24)—these are just a few examples of those who gained the attention of Heaven and obtained favor with God.

The summer home of Thomas Alva Edison is located in Fort Myers, Florida. Today it serves as a museum to display many of his inventions. One of his earliest inventions, the phonograph, can be seen here.

When you observe the phonograph, you can see teeth marks in the wood. As a lad, Thomas was running to catch a train when the conductor pulled him aboard by his ear. That incident left him hearing-impaired.

In order for Mr. Edison to know whether or not his invention worked, he bit into the wood and felt the vibration—the creator delighting in his creation.

God's yearning for man's adoration conveyed Him from Heaven to earth. Deity cloaked Himself in a robe of humanity and paid sin's penalty in order to hear praise's symphony. Instead of teeth marks we see nail prints—the Creator delighting in His creation.

The prerequisite that warrants His presence is not large crowds in stained-glass cathedrals. An IQ in the upper triple digits is not necessary. Instead we see a risen Savior comforting simple Mary—the Creator delighting in His creation.

One thing have I desired of the Lord, that will I seek after (Psalm 27:4a).

I have need of sustenance to survive in this world. I labor hard to provide for my family lest I should be an infidel. Responsibilities of this present life cannot be ignored, but nor can my obligation to God.

In this dog-eat-dog world it is easy to lose focus on things that matter most. The whirlwind of daily living has a way of subtly dominating our lives. Our commitment to Christ can slowly erode away unnoticed.

Desiring to better our standard of living is not a sin. However, new homes, new cars, new clothes, and better paying jobs place heavy demands on our time.

Religious politics and pleasing our peers are viable opponents to knowing Christ. The passion that motivated Mary Magdalene ought to be an incentive to us. Instead of worrying over who will be first and who will be last, we should strive to be first *and* last.

The last one at Calvary and the first to the tomb was granted a special visitation from the triumphant Christ. Mary was privileged with seeing God's "Sonrise." His appearance that day removed the threat of reliving yesterday.

Religious politics and pleasing our peers are viable opponents to knowing Christ. The passion that motivated Mary Magdalene ought to be an incentive to us.

I need various things, but one thing only justifies my utmost desire, and this is the one thing I will seek after. The apostle Paul articulated it well as he sat in a dank Roman dungeon, picked up the quill, and wrote the following:

But what things were gain to me, those I counted loss for Christ. Yea doubtless, and I count all things but loss for the excellency of the knowledge of Christ Jesus my Lord: for whom I have suffered the loss of all things, and do count them but dung, that I may win Christ, and be found in Him, not having mine own righteousness, which is of the law, but that which is through the faith of Christ, the righteousness which is of God by faith: that I may know Him, and the power of His resurrection, and the fellowship of His sufferings, being made conformable unto His death (Philippians 3:7-10).

Endnote

1. E.M. Bounds, *Power Through Prayer* (Grand Rapids, MI: Baker Book House, 1972), 49.

Chapter Three

The Compassionate Christ

In my distress I called upon the Lord, and cried unto my God:
He heard my voice out of His temple,
and my cry came before Him, even into His ears.
Psalm 18:6

What began as a beautiful sunny day turned into a rainy Friday evening. I was in North Carolina preaching a few nights for a good friend of mine, and the meeting seemed to be going quite well.

The pastor and I decided to leave town for a few hours to view some of the scenery. The time slipped away before we realized it, though, and soon the service was only a couple of hours away.

We made the short trip back to town and maneuvered our way through traffic in the pouring rain. The pastor expressed how he hoped that the weather did not deter his people from coming to church later on that evening.

As we talked I planned how I would take a quick shower, pull on my suit, and head for the church. *At least I'll have an hour or so to freshen up before the service begins*, I thought.

The Impassioned Soul

We were crossing the drawbridge when the light turned red, which was a bad sign for us. The bridge would be raised to allow the oncoming ship to pass, and we would be delayed for several minutes—time we could not afford to lose.

The ship seemed to take forever as it made its way under and past the bridge. I doubt if it really took any longer than usual, but with the service on our minds, it felt like a millennium.

I take preaching very seriously, and preparation time is important to me. If people are willing to sit and listen, then I feel an obligation to give them the best I have.

The captain of the ship carefully negotiated the vessel between the abutments, edging his way through the channel, ocean-bound. As the bridge slowly began to lower to its normal position, I breathed a sigh of relief. Suddenly it came to a stop. Then the traffic lights on the bridge went out. *What could have possibly happened?* we wondered. We sat staring at the bridge hoping that it was just some sort of brief power failure.

As it turned out, lightning had struck the upper portion of the bridge. It would take nearly an hour for it to be repaired. Needless to say, we were both fit to be tied.

I sat there in the car complaining about what I thought was a coincidence when this thought occurred to me: *What if this is not just a coincidence? Maybe the Lord has something to do with this.* You are probably thinking the same thing I was as I answered my curiosity, *What would the Lord have to do with lightning striking a bridge?*

The pastor and I stepped out of the car to inquire about what had happened. The lady in the car directly in front of ours said something to me in passing, so I stopped and we began to chat.

In the course of our short conversation, I told her that I was an evangelist visiting a local church and that it looked quite possible that

I was going to miss the evening service. She explained that she, too, was a Christian.

The pastor joined me at the lady's car, leaned into the window, and introduced himself. He gave a brief description of his church and where it was located. She informed us that she was waiting on the Lord concerning the church He would have her attend.

She then suggested that someone should pray for our dilemma, so the pastor volunteered. She followed with an optimistic prayer of how everything works for the good of those who love the Lord.

It was obvious that she was a nurse by the name tag on her jacket. She told of working on one of the mercy ships that is owned and operated by YWAM (Youth With A Mission) and expressed her desire to be used of the Lord.

I could sense that the Holy Spirit wanted to minister to this lady. As I listened to the two of them talk, I waited on the Lord for direction. Shoving everything else out of my mind, I tried to focus on what the Spirit was saying.

The lady then opened up some more and told of having a terrible week. She spoke of other trials she was going through and how she had desperately needed affirmation of the Lord's love for her.

The Holy Spirit began to minister. Specific events in her life were revealed, such as divorce. Her present husband's bondage also was revealed, and the Lord promised deliverance.

As the ministry continued, it was obvious that what was being said was correct. She begged us not to stop if the Lord had more for her. This woman was extremely hungry. As we spoke to her, it was almost like giving a starving child his first meal in days.

I will never forget the words she spoke in the middle of all this. "I am important; the Lord knew I desperately needed to hear from Him. He allowed all this to happen so I could meet you and be ministered to."

I came so close to missing this golden opportunity. Something was transpiring in the heavenlies, but I was frustrated by what was happening on the earth. My natural mind was dominating the spiritual mind.

While I thought the need waited for us at church, it sat directly in front of me. I was guilty of stepping over a need while looking for one.

Heaven Hears

In Second Timothy 4:2a Paul declares, "Be instant [be at hand] in season, out of season." I am sure that I have missed many opportunities to minister to hurting people by not discerning the moving of the Lord.

I have absolutely no problem believing that God, with all the important things He does, would allow lightning to strike a bridge, cause a major delay, and have traffic backed up for miles with people sitting in the rain aggravated over the situation. This was one of His children in dire need of help, and she gained instant priority.

The episode reminded me of blind Bartimaeus sitting by the wayside, begging. When Jesus was passing by, he began to cry out. Those around him told him to hush, telling him that Jesus had no time for him, when this was Jesus' whole purpose in coming to earth. (See Mark 10:46-52.)

> *The Spirit of the Lord is upon Me, because He hath anointed Me to preach the gospel to the poor; He hath sent Me to heal the brokenhearted, to preach deliverance to the captives, and recovering of sight to the blind, to set at liberty them that are bruised* (Luke 4:18).

Bartimaeus cried louder. "Thou Son of David, have mercy on me." Notice the next few words: "And Jesus stood still." (See Mark 10:48-49.)

We are not talking about some far-off deity who is harder to talk to than the President. This is the God who clothes the grass, arrays the lily, and feeds the sparrow (see Mt. 6:26-30). I might also add that He has the very hairs on your head numbered (see Mt. 10:30). His ear is always open to the cry of His children. In my mind, it was evident that He had shut everything down for the sake of this lady.

I believe we are much more important to God than we can ever realize. He so much wants to bless us and guide us through troublesome times. This lady had called, and Heaven answered. As it was with Bartimaeus, so it was with her.

A great man of God whom I esteem as a prophet once told me of an incident in his life. This particular event occurred in the1960's. He was on his way to an Oral Roberts meeting when the Lord spoke to him and told him that he and his wife would be sitting in the second row from the front. When they arrived at the huge auditorium, the only seats they found empty were halfway down the aisle from the platform.

After they were seated, he asked the Lord, "I thought You said I would be seated in the second row from the front?" Just a moment or two after he had whispered the question, an usher stopped at his seat. This man informed them of some empty seats in the second row and asked if they would like to move.

The next day in prayer he asked the Lord why He would take the time to tell him where he would be sitting at a miracle crusade. The Lord impressed this answer in his spirit: *Son, I know everything about you. I know where you are going to be and exactly what you will be doing. My eyes are ever upon you.*

In retrospect, I am sure that we all have had situations where the Lord did something special for us. It probably was not lightning striking a bridge, but it *is* just as spectacular: The Lord seemed to have gone out of His way to minister to us.

A very dear minister I know was at a major crossroads in his life. Not being able to sleep one night, he got dressed and went to the church. As he reached the church, he noticed a man sitting on the steps outside. As the pastor approached, the stranger looked up from where he was sitting and said, "I have been waiting for you." The young minister sat down beside this unexpected guest and was amazed as the man answered the questions racing through his mind.

Afterwards the stranger refused to let the pastor buy him breakfast, but he did allow the minister to drive him downtown. Almost as quick as he got out of the car, he disappeared.

I believe, as does this well-respected minister, that he experienced an angelic visitation. Today he is not only an esteemed minister of the gospel, he also is the leader of a large church organization.

If you are in need of an answer for some facet of your life, hold on—your answer is on the way. God will go to whatever measure needed to see that you receive it.

He hears the cry of the lonely wife struggling to raise the children on her own. The husband left her for someone younger, leaving her heart crushed. Her self-esteem has vanished. With mouths to feed and bills to pay, thinking no one cares, *He* comes near. A phone call, an unexpected check in the mailbox—something happens, and she realizes she is not alone.

Probably the most hopeless case in the New Testament is the demoniac who lived in Gadara. Mark 5:3-4 tells us that "no man could bind him, no, not with chains...neither could any man tame him." The Pharisees would be a more elite crowd to minister to, but they have no need of Him. He came to save the lost, not to mingle with the who's who (see Mk. 2:17).

I cannot picture the Lord sitting around with idle time on His hands if He lived in my city. Never has the world been in greater need than the present. Everywhere you turn, people are crying out in distress.

No Obstacle Is Too Big

The day has passed, and the shepherd leads the sheep back into the corral, out of harm's way. As they file through the gate, the shepherd takes count and finds one missing. Leaving the 99, he goes in search of the lost. When he finds the lost lamb, he places it on his shoulders and negotiates each step back to the fold so as not to injure it further.

Her net worth is ten pieces of silver. The amount may not seem very significant, but to her it certainly is. When she loses a coin, she lights a candle, sweeps the house, and seeks diligently until she finds it.

It's late at night as he paces the floor. Sleep has evaded him for several days. His mind is occupied with thoughts of his son. He did not hang a sign in the vacant bedroom window that read "Room for Rent" when the boy ran off. He tells the maid to go ahead and set the son's place at the table. He tells the farmhand to put that certain calf in the greenest part of the pasture.

When the prodigal finally comes home, Dad leaps off the front porch, runs to him, and kisses him. He is not about to sit casually by and watch the humbled son return. He places the ring on the son's finger and orders the best robe to be placed around his shoulders and shoes on his feet. (See Luke 15:4-24.)

It is obvious that Jesus was depicting His own character through these parables. The *agape* love of Christ will not allow Him to give up on anyone.

In his book, *When God Whispers Your Name*, Max Lucado tells of receiving a Christmas card several years ago with the following words:

> *If our greatest need had been information, God would have sent an educator. If our greatest need had been technology, God would have sent us a scientist. If our greatest need had been money, God would have sent us an economist. But since our greatest need was forgiveness, God sent us a savior.*[1]

No one has gone too far or sunk too deep for Him. Isaiah said, "Behold, the Lord's hand is not shortened, that it cannot save; neither His ear heavy, that it cannot hear" (Is. 59:1). Who does He have time for?

- A woman whose last name has changed five times with each new trip to the altar and who now is living "common-law" (Jn. 4:7-29).

- A tax collector who is so low down he would steal a preacher's Bible (Lk. 18:10-14).

- The adulteress in front of an angry mob anxious to stone her (Jn. 8:3-11).

- The drug addict whose arms are infested with needle holes.

- The inmate on death row awaiting his appointment with the executioner.

- A nurse in Wilmington, North Carolina, who desperately needs to feel the touch of her heavenly Father.

The Lord sees your plight and knows exactly what you are going through. Lightning may not be flashing, you may not be sitting in the company of an angel, but the Lord has a message for you. You may be reading it.

Determine in your heart that you are going to make it through whatever test or trial you are in right now. By God's grace you will overcome all obstacles and be victorious. He saw Moses on the backside of the desert; you are not out of His eyesight.

So I stopped worrying about the service. We knew very well that this was where the Lord wanted us. He had planned everything from the start, and all would be okay.

All who were present at that meeting at the drawbridge knew that something beyond coincidence had occurred. It seemed that when the lady had received exactly what she needed, the green light came on. The pastor and I drove home, got cleaned up, and went on to church.

There also is a common denominator in the three parables mentioned: rejoicing. As I came to the platform to minister, guess who was sitting in the congregation? The nurse, and what a service we had!

If the shepherd rejoiced more over finding the sheep that was lost than over the 99 that never did stray, if the woman had a party over the lost coin and the fatted calf was roasted for the prodigal son, then wait till Father gets you home!

I have never been to Heaven, but I feel safe in assuring you that we will not be disappointed. When we have walked through our last valley and climbed our final mountain, it will all be worth it.

Frank Lloyd Wright has never come close to designing anything comparable to what we will find there. Of all the splendor you will see, here are a few things you will *not* see: wheelchair ramps, handicap parking, ambulances, hospitals, police stations, and ghettos. There will be no burn wards where little children with charred skin cry for Mama.

When you pass through the pearly gates and stand in the presence of the Almighty, there are a couple of things I would like you to especially look for.

First, look for the rainbow round about the throne (see Rev. 4:3). It's God's promise; the storm is over. (See Genesis 9:11-15.) There will be no more wondering if the night will ever end. You will never again walk through life's deep valleys.

Second, pay close attention to what the Lord will present to you. It is a bottle filled with tears. Every time you were in pain or felt lonely or forsaken, He saw it (see Ps. 56:8). Better than that, He *felt* it. As each tear slid down your face, He cupped His hands and caught it.

Endnote

1. Max Lucado, *When God Whispers Your Name* (Dallas, TX: Word Publishing, 1994), 48.

Chapter Four

Not For Sale

And it came to pass after these things, that Naboth the Jezreelite had a vineyard, which was in Jezreel, hard by the palace of Ahab king of Samaria. And Ahab spake unto Naboth, saying, Give me thy vineyard, that I may have it for a garden of herbs, because it is near unto my house: and I will give thee for it a better vineyard than it; or, if it seem good to thee, I will give thee the worth of it in money. And Naboth said to Ahab, The Lord forbid it me, that I should give the inheritance of my fathers unto thee.
1 Kings 21:1-3

No other facts are offered about Naboth. The Bible does not tell us anything else other than he had a vineyard. We are not even told the acreage of this plot of real estate. Naboth may have been a man of means or he could have been a pauper.

I suppose it really doesn't matter what Naboth's status was when you put him in perspective to Ahab. Ahab was the king, and people in that position usually get what they want.

It appears that Ahab was in the middle of an expansion project. What he needed in order to finish it happened to belong to Naboth. It was the piece of land that bordered Ahab's property.

The presumptuous king approached Naboth and told him of his undertaking. He explained the new gardens and other details involved in the development.

"There is just one thing I lack to finish all this," declares Ahab. "The one thing I still need belongs to you, Naboth. It's the vineyard that sits next to my palace. Now, I know you are a reasonable man, and I feel certain that we can do business. I'm prepared to offer you the market value for your property. So we can settle this in one of two ways; it's up to you. I will give you another piece of land of the same value, or I can pay you in money."

The Mosaic Law forbade selling ancestral property unless one was in such a financial bind that there was no other alternative (see Lev. 25:23-28). If that did happen, in the year of jubilee it was to be restored back to the rightful owner (see Lev. 27:24).

Whether or not Naboth was in a financial crisis is anyone's guess. We do know that, regardless of his financial portfolio, he did not concede the land. The answer Naboth gave Ahab was one the king least expected. "The Lord forbid it me, that I should give the inheritance of my fathers unto thee."

The subject said no to the king. Average denied aristocracy. Ahab could not believe his ears. He was not accustomed to being denied what he wanted. What audacity, Naboth refusing Ahab!

Naboth's decision ultimately cost him his life. Ahab and Jezebel openly displayed contempt for God's law and acquired the vineyard through conspiracy (see 1 Kings 21:4-16).

One of the things that intrigues me most about this story is the value Naboth placed on his vineyard. The old cliché says that "every man has his price." Esau sold out for a bowl of pottage (see Gen.

25:29-34), Judas for 30 pieces of silver (see Mt. 26:14-16), and Demas for the present world (see 2 Tim. 4:10). Not so in this case.

I think it is important to understand how Naboth became the owner of the property. Another familiar cliché says, "Easy come, easy go." Naboth did not obtain the land through blood, sweat, and tears; his father willed it to him. The appreciation he had for something merited only due to lineage is commendable.

Preserving Our Priorities

The present generation is proof of what happens when the previous generation sells out. There are enormous consequences when values and morals decay. America's values are eroding so swiftly it is like a cancer-ridden body lying on a deathbed.

I know there is nothing holy about the American flag as a piece of material; however, it is a symbol that stands for freedom. The broad stripes represent the original 13 colonies. Each star represents a state in the union—a state located in one of the most blessed countries on the face of God's green earth, where freedom and democracy reign. How I desire to see this liberty preserved!

I am appalled when I see a picture of the star-spangled banner doused in gasoline and set ablaze. On the other side of the spectrum, watch the care employed by the war veteran as he lays the wreath at the foot of the monument, steps back, tilts his head, and salutes Old Glory. The explanation is quite simple. One understands the cost of freedom and has tremendous appreciation for it. The other knows nothing of foxholes and lying awake, not being able to catch a wink of sleep due to the constant firing of machine guns.

What we are witnessing in America today is a perverted sense of value. When I was growing up in New Brunswick, Canada, each year in elementary school I was given a pocket New Testament. It is unconstitutional to do this today in America. Instead students are handed a prophylactic. The rationale for this is "safe sex."

I am opposed to forcing religion on someone who chooses not to believe the way I do. However, I do not think this justifies our government in not making provision for the Ten Commandments to be posted on a wall in our schools. The overreaction to the "separation of church and state" has replaced prayer and Bibles with metal detectors in the entrances of America's schools.

When promiscuity is embraced rather than love for the family and commitment to the spouse, the innocent suffer. Children are caught in the crossfire and suffer the deepest wounds.

Sexual practices that are vehemently opposed in God's Word and that at one time were frowned upon by society are taught as alternative lifestyles. When one simply declares what the Bible has to say concerning this subject, he is branded a homophobe.

Just as abortion is an attack on the unborn child, so euthanasia is an attack on the elderly. The devaluing of human life is threatening the sanctity of America's youngest and oldest citizens. Somebody said it right: "Sometimes the most dangerous place for a child is in its mother's womb."

Virtue and chastity are combated by fornication. *Fidelity* and *monogamy* have become antiquated terms no longer applicable to today's society. When promiscuity is embraced rather than love for the family and commitment to the spouse, the innocent suffer. Children are caught in the crossfire and suffer the deepest wounds.

What happens when God's code of morals and ethics is forsaken? Broken homes, neglected children, cities infiltrated by gangs, widespread incurable disease, etc., are the results.

There must be a fixed standard in the universe. Without it ships would be lost at sea and a surveyor could never erect a transit. In these perilous days and changing times, something must remain the same. If not, humanity will be lost in a tumultuous sea of delusion and doomed to a Godless eternity.

Modern technology has produced a device known as the GPS (global positioning system). This is the device that was used in the Gulf War to guide smart bombs to Saddam Hussein's bunker. After the war, they were made available to the public, and now they can be purchased at the nearest department store for less than $200. Hunters and fishermen use the GPS to avoid getting lost in the woods. Pilots whose cockpits are outfitted with expensive navigation technology many times rely on this tiny device due to its incredible accuracy.

In these perilous days and changing times, something must remain the same. If not, humanity will be lost in a tumultuous sea of delusion and doomed to a Godless eternity.

I cannot help but ask this question: In man's quest to invent machinery to provide direction, why does he ignore ancient landmarks that have proven themselves throughout the ages? The one thing that will never change is the Word of God.

Pragmatism, doing what seems to work without regard to fixed principles of right and wrong, is largely in control. In both international and home affairs, expediency—at any price to maintain personal peace and affluence at the moment—is the excepted procedure. Absolute principles have little or no meaning in the place to which the decline of Western thought have come.[1]

It is imperative that we have something in our life that we place momentous value on, something so dear that the greatest arbitrator cannot persuade us into relinquishing it.

The warmth I encounter as I enter my home after being gone for several days on an evangelistic crusade is irreplaceable. The hugs and kisses that my two gorgeous daughters bestow on me are beyond monetary value. Holding my beautiful wife in my arms and hearing her whisper "I love you" is priceless.

Love, honor, respect, and integrity are virtues rather than gifts one is born with. If we come into possession of these great attributes, we will have earned them, not with dollars, but by establishing principles to live by and sticking to them regardless of how we might benefit otherwise.

Raise Your Price

It is not my objective to simply write about America's abandoning the faith of her founding fathers. Rather, I hope to convey a glimpse of God's love for His children and pray that all will feel a sense of self-worth.

God does not tolerate spiritual arrogance. James states very clearly that "God resisteth the proud, but giveth grace unto the humble" (Jas. 4:6b). However, a vast difference lies between self-esteem and being exalted in the flesh.

Humility is not something that debases us and demands that we think of ourselves as something worth less than a copper penny. It is extremely dangerous to believe that this is the definition of meekness. Those who do dare not pursue excellence for fear it will jeopardize their souls. God desires that we strive for greatness as we give Him glory.

It is not God's will for us to go through life feeling that we are worthless and nothing more than a liability to our heavenly Father. It is of utmost importance that we place great value on who and what we are. If we do not, it is quite possible that we will sell out for much less than we are worth.

The world does not heap accolades on the young people who maintain a disciplined lifestyle. Kids who carry handguns to school and rob classmates of their future will make the five o'clock news, but not "good" kids. It is shameful that good news is not newsworthy. In order for networks to maintain their viewership, they fill the news hour with gruesome scenes of unimaginable crimes.

When tempted to sell out, cherish your purity and esteem it highly. If it is worthless, why is satan so desperate for you to relinquish it? If you did surrender at some weak moment in the flesh, make a new consecration with the Lord right now.

A minister friend of mine tells the story of going to a yard sale and seeing a painting of Jesus. The price tag read $5. After a moment of pondering, he passed it up. The price was right, but he really wasn't impressed with the portrait.

An art collector happened to venture into the same yard sale. The painting that could have sold for $5 was appraised at $700,000. It made the headlines of the local newspaper.

For what shall it profit a man, if he shall gain the whole world, and lose his own soul? (Mark 8:36)

When I read this Scripture, I see a positive as well as a negative connotation. A person can acquire all the wealth of the world and live an extravagant life; however, if his soul is not right with God, all is in vain. What a waste. When the chasm is crossed from mortality to immortality, eternity will dawn with the realization that this is forever. Many who are presently clothed in the finest garments will appear naked in eternity.

Mark also is declaring that our soul is worth more than all the riches of the world. When the expense of redemption is considered, we have to believe that God must indeed love us. If our value could have been calculated in gold or silver, He would have exhausted Heaven's coffers. The price He paid far exceeded shekels of silver and bricks of gold. The thing that was most precious to Him, He gave.

For God so loved the world, that He gave His only begotten Son, that whosoever believeth in Him should not perish, but have everlasting life (John 3:16).

I confess that God did not happen on a bargain when He found me. I was the farthest thing from a glittering diamond or a precious stone. I was a worthless pebble lying on the floor of an ocean of iniquity and despair.

Hearken to Me, ye that follow after righteousness, ye that seek the Lord: look unto the rock whence ye are hewn, and to the hole of the pit whence ye are digged (Isaiah 51:1).

In God's mind He was not spending His effort on refuse. He saw something beyond scrap on the heap. As the saying goes, "One man's trash is another man's treasure."

Someone discovers treasure hidden in a field. A merchant man seeking goodly pearls finds one of great price. (See Matthew 13:44-46.) We are the treasure and the pearl. Upon being found, everything was sold to purchase us.

Fearfully and Wonderfully Made

For this cause I bow my knees unto the Father of our Lord Jesus Christ, of whom the whole family in heaven and earth is named (Ephesians 3:14-15).

Upon locating the perfect scenery and selecting the proper canvas, Pablo Picasso began to paint. If the finished project pleased him, he placed his name on it.

After carefully examining the wood and finding a piece that was flawless, Antonio Stradivari meticulously carved out a violin. Perfection had to be obtained before he endorsed it.

The greatest test of the ability of the creator is when the only material to work with is filled with flaws. What Picasso would have passed by and Stradivari would have discarded, God turned into a masterpiece.

It took only a few days to create the universe and all that is in it. The stars, sun, moons, and planets were spoken into existence. When it came to the creation of man, though, He reached down with His hands and fashioned us in His own image and likeness.

I've seen the beauty of the Rocky Mountains cloaked with virgin snow. I've gazed at the Niagara Falls and listened to its mighty cacophony. Azure skies of day are illuminated at evening by the brilliance of sunset's golden glow. Astronomers who peered into the heavens have beheld a fragment of the magnificence of God's playground.

What Picasso would have passed by and Stradivari would have discarded, God turned into a masterpiece.

Of all the beautiful things we have ever seen, none bear His name—except us, the redeemed of the Lord. We are His signature series. We were not produced in mass quantities on an assembly line; rather, we are handmade and endorsed by the Master Craftsman, proudly wearing a name greater than Monet, Rembrandt, or any other.

All through life you may have lived believing you were worthless. Perhaps what really added to this lack of self-esteem is that you were told you were an "accident"—not a planned pregnancy; just another mouth to feed.

The adopted child may not know who his biological parents are. He may struggle with rejection for his entire life—but, oh, he is special. The Bible declares that all have been fearfully and wonderfully made (see Ps. 139:14). There is not another you on the face of the earth.

Before mountains split the ocean's surface and reached toward the heavens, God saw each of us. In the intimate moments of our conception the Lord designed a plan for our life. Before we were even a thought, He knew our precise DNA structure (see Ps. 139). If we will come under His Lordship and walk in obedience to His Word, we can attain our God-given potential.

As individuals, we are sons and daughters; collectively, we are His Bride. Boaz was Ruth's kinsman-redeemer; Jesus is ours (see Ruth 3:13). Heaven's banquet room is ready; all is in order. One of these days He is going to come like a thief in the night and snatch us out of this world (see 1 Thess. 4:16–5:2).

I believe He did all this to make a statement. To express how much we mean to Him, He took the purest gold and used it as asphalt. He used 12 precious stones in the foundations and formed the gates of solid pearl (see Rev. 21:14-21). No need for the sun or moon or hydroelectric dams or nuclear generating stations. The radiance of His glory is sufficient.

The world may see us as a chunk of coal. But to our heavenly Father we are a sparkling diamond. The first time He came and took out the trash; next time He's coming for the jewels.

And they shall be Mine, saith the Lord of hosts, in that day when I make up My jewels; and I will spare them, as a man spareth his own son that serveth him (Malachi 3:17).

When satan comes and offers us all the wealth and pleasure the world can afford, we must tell him he has offended our self-worth. Besides, what makes him think we are for sale? We have already been purchased—not by corruptible things such as silver and gold, but by the precious blood of the Lamb (see 1 Pet. 1:18-19).

A Dog's Life

Step with me into the opulent dining hall of the royal palace. The golden candelabras emit a soft light, revealing a banquet fit for a king. Pleasant aromas ascend from the table, drifting gently through the air, suggesting how delectable the meal will taste. Notice the glimmering cutlery and golden chalices arranged meticulously at each setting. One cannot avoid seeing the exquisite artistry lining the walls, telling of past victories.

Seated at the table are Amnon, Tamar, Solomon, and Absalom. At the head of the table sits King David. But not an ounce of food is being consumed; it is not proper to begin eating when a chair remains empty.

As the waiting continues, the sound of shuffling feet is heard approaching the dining hall. Mephibosheth slowly drags his crippled feet along the plush carpet. His handicap is a constant reminder of the grace extended to him by the king.

For nearly 20 years he lived in Lodebar, which in Hebrew means a barren place, a place without pasture.[2] He was five years old when he suffered a fall, and he has been a cripple ever since. If King David were to follow that pattern set with his predecessors, Mephibosheth would have been executed. But instead of death David chooses life for Mephibosheth, and the lame boy moved into the big house.

Although he can be of no service to David, he gets to live here just the same. The others at the table were born to David; Mephibosheth is adopted. The story reminds us of ourselves. We had nothing to offer the Father, but He took us as we were. It wasn't what we could do for Him, but what He could do for us (see 2 Sam. 9; Rom. 8:15).

Disney has a point: All dogs can go to Heaven. Forget the orphaned puppy about to be put down. I am referring to those of us who once lived a dog's life but who moved from the pound to the palace!

It is not a mystical tale of a beautiful princess kissing an ugly frog and turning him into a prince. This miracle is much greater. The hand of God touches the heart of man and makes him a new creature.

Just as the potter remakes the vessel, so Jesus picks up a broken humanity ravaged by sin and transforms us into His children. Those who made an absolute disaster of their life fall on the mercy of Christ and are given a brand-new chance.

No Place Like Home

If by chance you slipped out the back door of Father's house and now find yourself in a pigpen, come on home. The devil can keep you there only as long as you allow him to convince you that you have no value.

The reason you have taken up residence with hogs and share their supper is you listened to the enemy. He told you that you were worthless. He relentlessly attacked your self-esteem simply because he knew a bargain when he saw one.

As he sat in the pigsty, the prodigal son put himself in perspective. The lowest person on Dad's payroll lived a whole lot better than he did. The farmhands who fed the slop to the hogs were not expected to eat it. The greatest night the son had on the road couldn't compare to the dullest day at Dad's place. Life on the outside was not all that it was cracked up to be (see Lk. 15:11-17).

David was a shepherd (see 1 Sam. 16:11); Saul herded goats (see 1 Sam. 9:1-3). I do not read anywhere that the Lord expected one of His own to live with swine. The passage in the Bible that mentions someone living with hogs is the story of the demoniac of Gadara. He was fighting a losing battle; he was destined to die in a cemetery when Jesus found him.

Everything about the sty speaks of sin and perversion. When you have reached the pigpen, you have reached the lowest level. The devil showed you dreams of stardom when all along he intended to dump you into the mire. The friend-turned-enemy never ever thought of you as anything more than a pig.

The devil has tried to convince you that coming home is complicated. It's actually quite simple. Turn around. The road that led you away will bring you back.

While you are hanging with hogs, back at home Dad is pacing the floor. His mind is constantly on you. When you packed up and pulled out, he didn't disown you. Everything is in place just as you left it, waiting for your return. For Heaven's sake, don't allow something so valuable to end up in the trash! Hurry on back.

The devil has tried to convince you that coming home is complicated. It's actually quite simple. Turn around. The road that led you away will bring you back. Don't let the smell of pig dung clinging to your body and the dirt ground beneath your nails keep you from coming home. Although you squandered the money Dad had set aside to provide an easier life for you, come on home. You wasted the money; please don't waste your life.

Your heavenly Father wants to remove the soiled rags from off your back and drape a clean robe around you. Those filthy garments are a constant reminder of your past. Let Dad pitch them in the fire, and they'll never remind you of your past again.

Come on home and soak in the cleansing flow of Calvary's crimson stream. Freshen up. There's a party about to be thrown in your name. It doesn't get any better than that.

Endnotes

1. Francis Schaeffer, *How Should We Then Live: The Rise and Decline of Western Thought and Culture* (Wheaton, IL: Crossway Books, 1983), 250-251.

2. James Strong, *Strong's Exhaustive Concordance of the Bible* (Nashville, TN: Crusade Bible Publishers, Inc., n.d.), #3810, 3808.

Chapter Five

Precious Pain

Now a certain man was sick, named Lazarus, of Bethany, the town of Mary and her sister Martha. (It was that Mary which anointed the Lord with ointment, and wiped His feet with her hair, whose brother Lazarus was sick.) Therefore his sisters sent unto Him, saying, Lord, behold, he whom Thou lovest is sick. When Jesus heard that, He said, This sickness is not unto death, but for the glory of God, that the Son of God might be glorified thereby. Now Jesus loved Martha, and her sister, and Lazarus. When He had heard therefore that he was sick, He abode two days still in the same place where He was.
John 11:1-6

It is evident after a brief examination of this Scripture passage that God was not upset with this household in Bethany; rather, He had a divine purpose in everything that occurred. John does an exceptional job at relating the story.

(It was that Mary which anointed the Lord with ointment, and wiped His feet with her hair, whose brother Lazarus was sick) (John 11:2).

Make no mistake about it. It was "that Mary," declared John. He pointed to her and explained this was the one who offered sacrificial worship, whose brother was sick.

Sometimes strange things happen to good people. The one we think deserves to be chastised is not always the person we see in pain. Some very good people have gone through some very rough times.

There is mixed emotion in serving God: pain and pleasure, ecstasy and agony. Whoever said Christianity was for people with low self-esteem and weak minds was terribly mistaken.

Christians today are not thrown to the mouths of hungry lions or cast into blazing furnaces. Today's warfare is, however, every bit as real. We all can testify that we have been in battle with the demons of hell and have walked through fiery trials.

Pain Is Not Forever

Recently a dear friend of mine wanted to know if God was angry with her. The reason she had this question in her mind was from her suffering with leukemia.

Approximately a year earlier, little eight-year-old Kelly had been diagnosed with this disease. After much prayer, the cancer went into remission. It appeared that she would get to enjoy a full life. Later we would learn this would not be the case. The cancer emerged from dormancy with a most horrible vengeance.

As we knelt on the floor beside her chair, my pastor and I both affirmed to this precious little girl that God was not upset with her. It was just the opposite. His love for her never wavered.

Service after service I watched this sweet family worship when it wasn't convenient. As Kelly sat on the pew, hardly able to move, Dad would stand with tears streaming down his face in adoration of his Lord. They did not get mad at God or accuse Him foolishly. Of course they questioned *why.*

Asking why is human. There is no sin in inquiring why trials come and why we have to face the situations that confront us. In His blood-covered, pain-ridden body Jesus looked into the heavens and asked why.

The Bible says it rains on the just and the unjust (see Mt. 5:45). Good and bad people are stricken with cancer. The Psalmist David declared, "Many are the afflictions of the righteous: but the Lord delivereth him out of them all" (Ps. 34:19). David did not say "from" but "out of." There is a major difference between the two.

The fact God still loved her was proven beyond any doubt early the next morning. I was on a plane bound for Canada while Kelly's family and pastor knelt at her side. Words were scarce from Kelly. Being subjected to pain of this magnitude, coupled with the treatment for the disease, left her absolutely exhausted.

Through it all this little warrior put up a tremendous fight. When all eyes were focused on her, she thought of others. On one of my family's earlier visits to see her, she gave my youngest daughter a cap. Kayla cherishes it to this day.

That morning, from a body wracked with pain, Kelly managed to squeeze out the words, "I see Jesus; He's coming for me." Those around her bedside admonished her to go and not linger for their sake. Releasing a loved one is not easy, but the task is much lighter when the final destination is considered.

In a moment it was over. Kelly's face had no expression as she lay lifeless. Those present wept over the emptiness. This petite and precious child left one enormous void.

After several minutes passed, the room was vacated except for the motionless body of the child who had brought so much sunshine into each of our lives. When her mom and dad returned to where Kelly lay, they were astonished at what they saw. A smile graced the countenance of darling little Kelly.

The Impassioned Soul

I have no answer as to why an adorable eight-year-old was taken from this life. I, along with everyone who knew her, wanted nothing less than her complete recovery. If there was a lack of faith, it certainly camouflaged itself well. This entire household possessed a strong love for God and a firm belief in His Word. Amid the emotions and the questions, her countenance spoke volumes.

When the news of her departure reached me and I was told of her smile, I remembered the words of our pastor. "Kelly, I promise you that you will not be in pain forever." God obviously had no ill feelings toward Kelly; the smile said it all: *Pastor, you were right. I'm not in pain anymore.*

> *They that sow in tears shall reap in joy. He that goeth forth and weepeth, bearing precious seed, shall doubtless come again with rejoicing, bringing his sheaves with him* (Psalm 126:5-6).

Notice that David did not say "they that sow *with* tears," but rather "*in* tears." That means sowing when it is not convenient, being faithful through times of pain and heartbreak. It implies squaring our shoulders and meeting the task head-on through life's storms and winds of adversity.

There is a reason as well as a reward for enduring such hardship. When all is said and done, we will have experienced a relationship with God we never had before. We never know Him as the Lily of the Valley until we trod through the deep, lonely valley (see Song 2:1). God could have spared the three Hebrew boys from having to enter a fiery furnace, but if He had, they would never have seen the fourth man (see Dan. 3:20-25).

We also will have an enormous harvest. The barns and silos will be teeming with joy. Tears of sorrow will vanish, and our joy will be full.

> *And let us not be weary in well doing: for in due season we shall reap, if we faint not* (Galatians 6:9).

All through life there is pain. There is the pain of childbirth and the pain in growing. Many have made their exit from this life in pain, only to cross the chasm from the temporal to that great eternal place where no pain is felt.

Look into the sparkling eyes of a little girl. She dreams of being a ballerina. But before she dances with grace, she will practice in pain. We can endure pain more easily when there is a purpose for it.

Pain can be precious. A mother thinks so when she beholds the beauty of the newborn. It is worth it to the lad who has become strong and tall—as well as to the person who knows Jesus as his Savior, when he is ushered by an entourage of angels into the presence of the King.

Look Up, Not Down

Therefore his sisters sent unto Him, saying, Lord, behold, he whom Thou lovest is sick (John 11:3).

An exclamation or a question mark could be placed at the end of that statement. They are surprised that the one loved by the Master is sick. "Jesus, the one You love is sick? If You love him, why is he suffering?"

I am an advocate of praying for divine health and have been blessed by witnessing miracles of healing. Several times in my own life the Lord's healing virtue has been released, bringing a speedy if not instant recovery. However, after living for God for any length of time, we learn that being His children does not exempt us from suffering.

...after living for God for any length of time, we learn that being His children does not exempt us from suffering.

Mary and Martha were chosen by God to experience grief and heartache. Their minds were blown and their hearts broken at their brother's death. "Weeping may endure for a night, but joy cometh in the morning" (Ps. 30:5b).

The Impassioned Soul

Sometimes it requires all our effort to last through the darkness of night. Perhaps you are in the proverbial nighttime of your life. Things have taken a drastic shift; everything has changed from "going great" to collapsing around you. Instead of days of sunshine and laughter you find yourself in a downpour of despair.

You toss and turn and wonder if the sun will ever shine again. You sincerely want to believe, but you are overwhelmed with doubt because of the continual onslaught of the enemy.

Then somewhere amid the restlessness you hear the chirping of a bird. Another answers. Soon the chirping turns into a song, and once again tiny creatures raise their beaks toward heaven in praise of the Creator.

As the sun slowly begins to rise in the east, rays of light beam through the window of your soul and you feel the warmth of a brand-new day. You know that it is over. Nighttime does not last forever, and neither do trials.

Growing up in eastern Canada where the winters can be fierce from the bitter cold that seems to last an eternity, springtime was my favorite season. When winter turned monotonous, spring gave us something to look forward to.

An important key to a successful climb is to never look down. Instead, fasten your gaze upon the goal.

Springtime meant that bicycles, stored in the woodshed, could be brought back out to enjoy. Heavy coats, gloves, and caps would be stowed at the back of the closet. Windbreakers and running shoes became the proper attire.

Even the smell of spring was a welcoming agent. It was the season for new life to begin. Frozen ground covered with snow would soon give way to green grass and delightful flowers. Birds that had taken shelter in warmer climates would return.

If you could catch a glimpse of what awaits you at the top of the mountain, you would labor with all that is within you to scale the summit. An important key to a successful climb is to never look down. Instead, fasten your gaze upon the goal.

There are several things in common with each time the disciples got into a ship and set sail (see Mk. 4–5):

- The multitudes were sent away.

- They were confronted with storms.

- No one was lost at sea.

- Great miracles happened when they arrived on the other shore.

If you find yourself in rough waters, take consolation in the fact that you have been selected for the storm. Others will enjoy the loaves and fishes, but then they will be sent away (see Mk. 4). An invitation has been extended to you. Jesus knows there is a storm brewing, and He wants you in it. It is not His motive to terrify you at sea; He has peace that passes human logic, and He wants to impart it to you (see Jn. 14:27; Phil. 4:7).

Whenever you endeavor to do something for the Kingdom of God, ill winds of adversity will blow and the devil will try everything in his power to stop you. You are a person with a mission destined to do damage to the kingdom of darkness, and he will not take that sitting down.

Decide that you will make it. The belly of the boat may be full of water and the timbers snapping like twigs, but you're going to make it. The memories of the storm will pale in comparison to the joy that welcomes you on the other side. Before long the tumultuous waves and howling winds will be at your back and sweet victory just ahead.

A Higher Purpose

When Jesus heard that, He said, This sickness is not unto death, but for the glory of God, that the Son of God might be glorified thereby (John 11:4).

The Impassioned Soul

Our Lord's main objective was not to travel to Bethany and show them a miracle; rather, He wanted to show them glory. This revelation would not be a shallow or mere strip of veneer; it would not be glitter or glamour, but glory.

We sell ourselves short by not waiting on the Lord and permitting Him to have preeminence. We enjoy our encounters with God, but before long we reach a plateau. His desire is to take us from glory to glory. Amid the lethargy and apathy, God yearns to have a relationship with us.

This is not to imply that miracles are nothing but insignificant manifestations of power. When we experience the supernatural intervention of our Lord, it is a direct result of His love and compassion for us.

In the situation with Mary, Martha, and Lazarus, Jesus wanted to convey to them that He is Lord of all. What appeared to be a setback was actually a setup. If satan had sought this as an occasion to use for evil purposes, God certainly turned the tables on him. Mary and Martha were destined to be victors, not victims.

Now Jesus loved Martha, and her sister, and Lazarus (John 11:5).

The apostle John reiterated the fact that Jesus loved these people. This entire ordeal was not orchestrated so that deep, hidden sin would be brought to the surface. No, this was an act of love, not anger.

When He had heard therefore that he was sick, He abode two days still in the same place where He was (John 11:6).

It is important to remember that Jesus was a man subject to like passion (see Heb. 4:15). He has just received word that His friend was sick. Our first impulse would be to rush to the bedside of Lazarus and smite the affliction. However, that was not the plan of the heavenly Father. God's desire was to manifest Himself beyond what they had already experienced.

70

Mary and Martha have witnessed Jesus healing the sick. They have attended His crusades and watched as crippled limbs were straightened. Eyes that had never captured the brilliance of sunlight and ears that had never heard a child's laughter suddenly were opened.

Before glory is revealed, pain will be felt. Tomorrow they would know that God is never too late; today they wonder where He is.

Before glory is revealed, pain will be felt. Tomorrow they would know that God is never too late; today they wonder where He is. If you will permit Him, God will be all things to you. Your part is to be willing to be placed in the situation that warrants the manifestation of God.

It is easy to allow yourself to feel forsaken by God when an area of your life is tested. Jesus gave you a promise, though, that He would never forsake you (see Heb. 13:5). The time when you feel that God is nowhere to be found is when He is the closest, for in those times you are not walking by feeling but by faith.

Notice that Shadrach, Meshach, and Abednego did not find the fourth man in the king's court or chambers. They found Him in the furnace (see Dan. 3:25). John the Revelator noticed something about the feet of Jesus:

> *His head and His hairs were white like wool, as white as snow; and His eyes were as a flame of fire; and His feet like unto fine brass, as if they burned in a furnace; and His voice as the sound of many waters* (Revelation 1:14-15).

Mary and Martha worked frantically to sustain the life of their beloved brother. But his hands grew clammy, and his face was chalk white. There was a death rattle in his throat, and he slipped in and out of consciousness.

The confidence of these ladies could not be shaken. Their faith was rock solid. They believed that Jesus was on His way. At the right moment He would appear, and the sickbed would be emptied of the patient.

Mary and Martha comforted each other with the words that He had reportedly said: "This sickness is not unto death" (Jn. 11:4). "He's not going to die. Life may be fleeing, but it will not vanish."

It's Not Over Till It's Over

Then the unexplainable occurred. Lazarus died. He was moved from the cot to the coffin. What then do you tell someone who had invested such trust and stood with such faith?

Not only was their brother dead, their faith was wounded. The Jesus they lifted up had let them down. Remember which Mary this was? She was the one who broke open the ointment, and now He had broken her heart.

Does this story remind you of your own? The devil enjoys pouncing on people who have given all and seem to have nothing in return. You tithe faithfully, and whenever a special need arises and the request is made, you dig a little deeper. But instead of blessings, all you have are bills. Never forget—when you are down to nothing, God is up to something.

Before the deceased was placed in the tomb, two sisters with eyes stained with tears surveyed the crowd at the graveside. No Jesus. If there was to be no cure, how about a little comfort? They were not expecting miracles at that point, but a soothing word and a strong shoulder would have been better than boycotting the burial.

Our friend Lazarus sleepeth; but I go, that I may awake him out of sleep (John 11:11b).

The mountain had just been reduced to a molehill. Through the power of His word, Jesus disarmed death. Whether it is cancer or a headache, whether you are in the grave or in bed, it makes no difference to Him.

No situation is beyond the grasp of God. While you are in panic, God is at peace. They will sweat and move the stone; He will speak and move death.

The situation that threatens to finish you off is not causing as much as one bead of perspiration on the brow of Christ. Instead of becoming history, you will make history. The thing that should bury you instead will bless you.

Lazarus, come forth (John 11:43c).

The scene changed drastically at Bethany that day. Lamenting turned to laughter. Mary and Martha's understanding of Jesus was enlightened. He no longer was simply a healer. These ladies thought resurrection was something in the distant future; now they know it is a Person staring them in the face.

So it will happen to you. He will come right on time, bare His mighty right arm of power, and show Himself to be Lord of all. Hold on, dear child. There is a new day dawning.

Do you feel a quickening in your soul? Let me explain what you are experiencing. Darkness is fleeing, and the sun is rising. Joy is rapidly approaching. Resurrection power is making its way to your cemetery of broken dreams.

Your eyes will behold Him from a perspective that you never had in the past. Whatever you saw Him as, that much more is He becoming.

At one time you thought the final chapter of your life would end in defeat. Instead of falling into an abyss of despair, you now are being elevated to brand-new heights. In John 11 it appeared that Mary and Martha had enjoyed their last meal together with their brother. Not so. Read chapter 12. As the saying goes, "It's not over till it's over."

Chapter Six

Brokenness

And as they were eating, Jesus took bread, and blessed it,
and brake it, and gave it to the disciples, and said,
Take, eat; this is My body. And He took the cup, and
gave thanks, and gave it to them, saying, Drink ye all
of it; for this is My blood of the new testament, which is
shed for many for the remission of sins.
Matthew 26:26-28

In the mid-1970's, a minister friend of mine went to Seoul, Korea. While there he decided to visit what would later become the world's largest church. When he arrived at the construction site, he saw nothing that even hinted of having the potential of what it is today. A cement slab with steel girders covered with bird dung was all that could be seen.

Construction on the mammoth auditorium had come to a grinding halt. The pastor of the church, Dr. Cho, was engaged in a fierce attack with the forces of darkness, and it looked as though satan would win.

As he walked across the cement, he noticed an elderly Korean man guarding the property. "It looks as though Dr. Cho's ministry has come to a screeching halt," remarked my friend. "Oh no," replied the guard. "God is breaking Dr. Cho. When God is through with him, he will rise higher and stronger."

Dr. Cho's mother-in-law entered an extensive time of prayer and fasting for her son-in-law, and God intervened. Dr. Cho returned to the pulpit with renewed vision and strength.

In 1991 I had the privilege of attending this enormous church, which has reached a membership of more than 700,000. I was totally awestruck at what I observed there.

It seems that the one whom God bruises, He uses. The ones who bless you the most are the ones who have bled the most.

It seems that the one whom God bruises, He uses. The ones who bless you the most are the ones who have bled the most. Read the biographies of the men and women chosen to be vanguards of revival, and you will detect a common thread. Whether physically or spiritually, they all endured some degree of suffering.

The Place of Surrender

I am not suggesting that anyone other than Christ has attained sin-remitting power as a result of their bleeding. The blood of Jesus, the only true Lamb of God, alone possesses this power. However, there are those who have allowed the Lord to bring them to a place of surrender where He can use them to bless others and bring glory to Him.

After Jesus fasted in the wilderness, He was confronted by the devil. Satan showed Jesus all the kingdoms of the world and tempted Him, saying, "All these things will I give Thee, if Thou wilt fall down and worship me" (Mt. 4:9b). Satan suggested that he would relinquish every captive as long as Christ would avoid Calvary (see Mt. 4:1-11).

There are no shortcuts in the Kingdom of God. Without the shedding of blood there is no remission (see Heb. 9:22). Jesus fully understood His mission and every horrid detail it involved. His body would be bruised, crushed, and broken. Blood would pour from His side like water from a sieve, separating life from the body.

Satan will place anything and everything in your pathway to get you to make a detour around the cross. He has got to stop you from having a bloody encounter at Calvary. Why? A man who has not fallen on the rock and been broken is absolutely no threat to the devil.

As a young pastor in Canada, I was placed on the potter's wheel—and the breaking process began. The very thing I was so eager to enter, I found myself wanting to escape.

After pastoring for only a few months, my opinion of the ministry quickly changed. This was service, not stardom. Through this time I gained a healthy respect and deep appreciation for the pastors who had sown into my life.

Since childhood my passion was to minister to the sick and to travel the world and witness multitudes being liberated from sin and sickness through the power of the Holy Spirit. More than a desire, it was almost an obsession. It was my destiny to be an evangelist.

In my journey to arrive at that point, I had to pass through the sheepfold. Through this process a compassion for people was imbedded deep within my heart. If in the past I possessed ulterior motives, this was the catalyst that produced pure ones.

Although there would come a time when the Lord would miraculously supply the finances for airfare to minister overseas, at this time I simply needed Him to provide fuel for our car to get us to church.

In those early years of ministry, my wife and I learned what it was to trust in the Lord for all things. One time when company was coming for the weekend and there wasn't enough food, we prayed. Within an hour, one of the young ladies in the church who was a new convert showed up at our door. She said the Lord impressed her to bring the pastor a box of groceries.

Today you face lions and bears; tomorrow there are giants. The lesson to be learned is that whenever you engage in warfare, you do it for the life of the sheep, not for accolades from your peers. If you are addicted to affirmation from people, your ministry will be short-lived.

In retrospect, I understand how the Lord used this time to develop and mature His call on my life. Many times I questioned whether or not I was even called of God. I must have told the Lord at least a thousand times that I wanted to be released from the ministry, only to bury my face in the carpet and repent five minutes later.

While my spirit loved it, my flesh loathed the breaking process. Pride was weakening and the anointing was increasing. Morton finally surrendered. I released myself from the fleshly prison of carnal ambitions to live in freedom and follow the Spirit.

An overwhelming desire to help others throbbed in my heart. Now I would march to the beat of His drum. I would gladly minister to the teeming masses in distant lands or to a handful in a tiny hamlet in eastern Canada.

The breaking process continued even after I resigned from the pastorate. My wife and I moved from our quaint community, believing that we were following the leading of the Spirit.

For the next several months I sat idle, not knowing where to go or what to do. To imply that finances were scarce would be an understatement. One of the feelings that haunted me the most was that of being an infidel in not providing for my family.

At this juncture in our lives the Lord blessed us with our first child. I vividly remember the day Marilyn received the news that we were going to have a child. Since we were not much more than children ourselves, and due to the pressing circumstances, we accepted the fact with mixed emotions. Welcoming a baby into our lives was not the reason for hesitancy. How in the world we would provide for it was.

As I write about this, I am still overwhelmed with emotion. It was a time in my life when I never had felt so helpless, yet had experienced a peace that exceeded my reasoning. In the innermost chambers of my spirit I knew I was called of God and that He would supply every need.

On August 9, 1984, Datha-Jo Lynne Bustard fought her way into this world and became a part of our lives. Had she the opportunity to see and understand what she was coming to, she might have opted otherwise.

One day during that time I sat at the dinette in the kitchen of our tiny apartment and began to weep—not for pity but for praise. Rather than complain, I offered thanks to the Lord for His goodness to my family. Invisible arms embraced me, and I felt as though I were one of the wealthiest people on the planet.

I have compartmentalized my memories of those days. The negative ones have been trashed and the positive ones filed away in albums in my mind. It does me a world of good whenever I review these special times. In all honesty I have no desire to relive them, but I would not trade them for anything.

I do not wish to imply that I have had to endure things no one else has. We do each other a terrible injustice by comparing our trials. What may devastate me might not so much as move another, and vice versa. We all have had our share of rough roads to travel. My hope is that my experience will encourage someone else who is in the vise and feeling the pressure.

Every person who has ever accomplished anything substantial in the Kingdom of God shares a common denominator. They have been broken. That is the reason God trusted them with the task.

Death Brings Fruit

Many times I prepare to preach a sermon; a few times I have been prepared for the sermon. The difference is living and experiencing the subject matter. The deepest form of communication is *symphono*. All parties involved are in perfect harmony and are able to empathize with one another.

It is not our excellent enunciation that captivates the listener, but the realization that we know from whence we speak. Allow me to paraphrase a prophet: We sat where they sat (see Ezek. 3:15). Borrowing from modern lingo: "Been there, done that."

Before Jesus climbed Calvary's hill, He entered Gethsemane's garden. In a few hours He would pour blood; now He would sweat it (see Mt. 26:36; Mk. 14:32; Lk. 22:39-44). His back would be beaten, His body bruised.

Gethsemane means "oil press."[1] In the Old Testament, the lamp that burned in the temple was fueled with pure olive oil that was *beaten*. It was not enough to squeeze the olive; the it had to be pulverized.

> *It is not our excellent enunciation that captivates the listener, but the realization that we know from whence we speak.*

Isaiah said, "It pleased the Lord to bruise Him" (Is. 53:10). The Hebrew word for "bruise" in this passage is *daka*, which means to beat to pieces, break, crush, destroy.[2] Through this God knew that deliverance would come to the captives. The body of Jesus would have to break and bleed for humanity to be blessed.

The process of crushing allows a grape to attain its finest potential. It also will liberate the most beautiful fragrance of a rose. Pressure applied today will release potential tomorrow.

The greatest achievement of our Lord was not resurrecting Lazarus, but Himself. Emptying the grave was one thing. Entering it was another.

God took pleasure in allowing His Son to be bruised and put to death (see Is. 53:10). The ultimate sacrifice of Heaven gave birth to a glorious Church that spans the globe.

Christ's death and resurrection damaged satan's kingdom beyond repair. It was the last time hell's gatekeepers remember seeing the keys to the front doors. The grave lost its sting; death lost its victory (see 1 Cor. 15:55). All humanity was granted a pardon from sin's prison.

Verily, verily, I say unto you, Except a corn of wheat fall into the ground and die, it abideth alone: but if it die, it bringeth forth much fruit (John 12:24).

Something emanates from deep within the very core of the spirit of one who is broken before the Lord. To be anointed by the Holy Spirit and witness the supernatural power of the Lord is marvelous. To kneel at His feet and be of a contrite heart is essential.

I once was given a tour of new office facilities that a friend of mine had just leased. I noticed scratches on the conference table—a beautiful piece of furniture that had been custom-built for the room. When I pointed them out to him, he did not express any disappointment in the workmanship. Instead he replied, "That just gives it character."

It would be nearly impossible to write of brokenness and not refer to Jacob, the man who got a death grip on God and experienced a transformation.

Jacob's life had been one filled with deception. Each passing day was lived looking over his shoulder, knowing that sooner or later the odds would catch up. Then came they day he would rather reconcile with God and die at the hands of Esau than go on living a life that was nothing more than a mere existence.

The one who was a character now possessed character. Jacob, now called Israel, hobbled from Jabbok a new man. The irregular gait originated from a wrestling match with the Lord.

The scar on his hip and the limp in his walk were permanent reminders of the touch of God. Every time Jacob took a step, he remembered when his walk was swift but his heart wicked (see Gen. 32).

It took him 20 years to go from the pit to the palace, but Joseph clung to his dream and saw it fulfilled. In one day he was delivered from the dungeon and placed over the storehouses of Egypt.

Every time Jacob took a step, he remembered when his walk was swift but his heart wicked.

The brothers who sold him came to buy from him. As he stood before them, he was faced with a decision. Should he deal corn or deal revenge? The power of life and death were in the palm of his hand.

Rather than be overcome with anger, he was overwhelmed with love. Joseph understood this to be the divine plan of God. Rather than blame his brothers, he gave credit to God:

> *And Joseph said unto his brethren, Come near to me, I pray you. And they came near. And he said, I am Joseph your brother, whom ye sold into Egypt. Now therefore be not grieved, nor angry with yourselves, that ye sold me hither: for God did send me before you to preserve life* (Genesis 45:4-5).

David became a hero one day and then fled for his life the next. Between the sheepcote and the throne there were 15 years filled with disappointment and heartache (see 1 Sam. 17–19; 2 Sam. 5:4).

After David decapitated Goliath, Saul recruited him to head up his military. That was quite a major lifestyle change; he went from the pasture to the palace. Quite a promotion for a lad who was not voted most likely to succeed! When the prophet Samuel was sent to the house of Jesse to anoint the next king over Israel, David's brothers were invited, but not him. Evidently his own dad never thought of David in terms of amounting to anything more than a shepherd (see 1 Sam. 16:11).

David's days of living in luxury were short-lived in the beginning. God allowed him to experience royalty, prosperity, and nobility before giving him a crash course in humility.

Jonathan, Saul's son and David's best friend, told David of his father's plan to assassinate him. Thus David did not attend the royal feast but stood in the shadow of the forest by the rock of Ezel, which means "rock of departure."[3] Jonathan would shoot three arrows into the air. If the arrows landed nearby, it was safe for David to return. If they went beyond the rock, David would know that he must flee for his life.

Neither of the three arrows landed at David's feet. So he bade farewell to his friend—and Jonathan returned to the city alone (see 1 Sam. 20). That night David would sleep in a cave, not a castle. For how long he would be on the lam, he really did not know. One thing David was certain of, though: If God could take him from the sheepcote to the palace (if even for a few short days), then He can place him on the throne.

David's days of living in luxury were short-lived in the beginning. God allowed him to experience royalty, prosperity, and nobility before giving him a crash course in humility.

Had David ordered his own steps and returned to the palace, avoiding the breaking process, he might have made it through the door, but never to the throne. Instead, the Saul who sought his life would be instrumental in destroying any similar traits found within David.

One night as his archenemy slept, David stood over him with sword in hand. However, he cut only Saul's robe, not his flesh. Years later, when David heard that Saul was dead, he mourned rather than rejoiced (see 1 Sam. 26:7-9; 2 Sam. 1:5-12).

Joseph and David both were shown the end from the beginning; it was an incentive that helped them endure days of despair when they felt forgotten and forsaken.

Broken and Released

As a boy I was embarrassed to share with anyone the dreams and visions I had, lest they should make light of them and discourage me. Endless hours of mental movies played through my mind. I beheld the lame walking, the dumb talking, and the blind seeing.

I cannot tell you exactly how many years there were between the first dream and the first miracle. I can tell you that, in the midst, many times I wondered if those dreams would ever be fulfilled.

It is imperative that we understand the working of God. He will allow us to be confronted with circumstances that will make us or break us. Michal Eyquem de Montaigne said, "We are not so much affected by what happens as we are by our attitude of what has happened."[4] Our perception of a situation determines the outcome.

We can allow ourselves to be absorbed in self-pity, thinking we are expected to endure situations no other will encounter. Or we can say as Job did, "When He hath tried me, I shall come forth as gold" (Job 23:10b).

The devil will offer you anything as long as you will avoid your appointment with the Potter. You need to make the decision of where you want to be: the potter's wheel or the potter's field. The latter is filled with those who thought it was possible to be blessed without being broken.

Gideon stepped outside the camp with his army of 300 men. Armed with a pitcher in their left hand and a trumpet in their right, they faced the Midianites, who outnumbered them more than a thousand to one.

Notice what the Bible said concerning the pitchers:

And he divided the three hundred men into three companies, and he put a trumpet in every man's hand, with empty pitchers, and lamps within the pitchers (Judges 7:16).

They emptied the pitchers of everything and placed a candle inside. When the trumpets were blown and the pitchers were *broken*, the enemy fled for their lives. The smashing of clay released the glow of the candle. Gideon's army exposed themselves and struck terror in the hearts of the enemy (see Judg. 7).

It is of absolute importance to be filled with the Holy Spirit. The battle we are engaged in is spiritual, not physical. Having a positive attitude in a negative society is beneficial; being filled with God's power is crucial.

We pose very little threat to the forces of evil while the vessel remains intact. However, we could experience a revival of cataclysmic proportions if we Spirit-filled Christians would rend the vessel.

When vessels shatter, hell will shudder. If the hand of God ever penetrates the veil of flesh surrounding your spirit, it will release a soldier destined to do damage to the powers of darkness.

When we smash the ornate alabaster containers and release the incense of sacrificial praise, we will be catapulted to spiritual heights unlike anything we have ever experienced. Mundane songs sung by sleepy saints will transform into vibrant worship choruses. We do not lack modern keyboards and lively lyrics; the missing element is the participation of our spirits, not just our mouths.

Then brokenness will give way to blessing. Church services that have degenerated to the gathering of the grumpy will once again possess vitality and excitement. Revivals we had heard of will be repeated, only this time bigger and better.

Unity will return to the Body of Christ. Renewed strength and vision will come to God's people. The winds of the Holy Spirit will blow and, from the valley where once dry bones lay, a mighty army will emerge.

Life in the Spirit will cost you death to the flesh. If you are offered a deal on power any other way, rebuke the salesman. His pitch may be smooth, but his product is phony.

Endnotes

1. James Strong, *Strong's Exhaustive Concordance of the Bible* (Nashville, TN: Crusade Bible Publishers, Inc., n.d.), #1068.

2. *Strong's Exhaustive Concordance of the Bible*, # 1792.

3. *Strong's Exhaustive Concordance of the Bible*, # 237.

4. As quoted in Dorothy Carnegie, ed., *Dale Carnegie's Scrapbook: A Treasury of the Wisdom of the Ages* (New York: Simon and Schuster, 1959), 91.

Chapter Seven

Continuing

These all continued with one accord in prayer and
supplication, with the women, and Mary the
mother of Jesus, and with His brethren.
Acts 1:14

It is impossible to define the love of God. I can offer a Greek word, *agape*, which speaks of infinite, incessant affection. However, this certainly does not encompass the passion that a holy God has for sinful man.

In order for someone to furnish a definition of God's love, he would have to know how far it is from Heaven to earth. How many light-years did the journey take? Paul said there are at least three heavens (see 2 Cor. 12:2), so even if it were possible to determine the distance, the question remains unanswered.

It goes beyond using complicated computers and far-reaching telescopes to provide a figure that would give us some idea of the distance. How far is it from God to an angel? It is a case of comparing apples and oranges. How do you measure condescension, such as God to an angel?

This inconceivable journey to purchase our salvation brought God lower than an angel. The Lord, who is rich in mercy, spanned the incredible chasm and became man.

To liken this wondrous event to that of a king becoming a peasant is a gross injustice. It is one thing for a monarch to be dethroned or for a president to be voted out of office or impeached. But the Lord voluntarily disrobed Himself of splendor and took upon Himself the likeness of sinful flesh (see Rom. 8:3; Phil. 2:5-8).

Charles Spurgeon once said:

Go and measure heaven, weigh the mountains in scales, take the ocean's water and count each drop, and count the sand upon the sea's wide shore. When you have accomplished all of this, you can tell me how much He loves you.

A Price to Pay

God was not the only key player involved, however. Just as redemption required a compassionate God, it also demanded a virtuous woman. The prophet Isaiah declared: "Therefore the Lord Himself shall give you a sign; Behold, a virgin shall conceive, and bear a son, and shall call His name Immanuel" (Is. 7:14). The phrase "a virgin shall conceive" expresses volumes.

Here was a woman who had maintained an immaculate reputation. Her demeanor spoke of purity. Mary conducted herself in a way that demanded respect. She found favor with God and was blessed among women—an honor bestowed upon no other person—to become the mother of Christ.

Nothing compares with being used of the Lord. For God to place His anointing on you and call you to His service is beyond anything you can ever experience.

Everything has its price, though, and being used of the Lord is no exception. Mary was espoused to Joseph. Although the consummation of the marriage had not yet occurred, they were legally bound (see Mt. 1:18). What if people were to misjudge her? The penalty she faced was the same as for one who had committed adultery—death (see Lev. 20:10).

Not only was her good name tarnished, but she also faced the possibility of death. The Mosaic Law said that adulterers were to be stoned. If the Pharisees were to stone her, they would destroy what God was doing.

This was precisely why Joseph sought to "put her away" (Mt. 1:19). This does not imply that he sought to place her in confinement. It went far beyond sheltering her from tongues wagging over a hot piece of gossip. Joseph wanted to *sever* the relationship. Mary had just announced to him that she was impregnated by the Holy Ghost. There was no precedent established for that ever happening before. It is not difficult to understand Joseph's wanting to end the relationship.

This precious, undefiled lady was investing her life to fulfill the purpose for which God had chosen her. Anything of value does not come cheap.

Being used of the Lord does not mean you won't be misunderstood. Mary knew that this was a holy thing. It was not a situation where a young lady had been overcome with lust and had a fling.

This young lady had an encounter with God. Her head would not hang low in shame. The holy Child within dispelled the guilt without.

Some would judge her harshly and look upon her with disdain. Others would forever have a question mark in their mind as they wondered what really happened. This young lady had an encounter with God. Her head would not hang low in shame. The holy Child within dispelled the guilt without.

History testifies that when people lay their reputations on the altar and ignore the pressure from peers, revival occurs. I am not suggesting that everyone who has a bizarre idea has heard from Heaven; however, we must exercise caution when we hear of happenings in the Church that we do not understand, lest we speak against God.

The Impassioned Soul

Mary carried the baby in her womb, eagerly awaiting the day when she would carry Him in her arms. The overwhelming joy an expectant mother feels—as well as the pain—was realized. The upset stomach and swollen legs produced days filled with anxiety and nights void of rest.

Then the time for Light to enter darkness arrived. The moment for Truth had finally come. The delivery room was a damp stable in a cave, not a cozy room in the inn. Jesus would not lie on a mattress stuffed with feathers but in a manger filled with straw (see Lk. 2:7).

We are not promised the most comfortable environment when ministering for our Lord. Some of the greatest revivals were birthed in the crudest of circumstance.

For the missionaries who labor in Third World countries—forsaking family, friends, and modern conveniences to heed the heavenly call—it would be so much easier to stay at home. There must be those who are willing to be put out so others can be let in.

The contractions came more frequently, and the labor pains were unbearable. Joseph, kneeling at her side, gently wiped the beads of sweat from her brow. He assured Mary that everything would be all right as she desperately clung to his hand.

Then it happened! The greatest event of all the ages: Jesus was born! Amid the lowing of oxen came the cry of a baby. Heaven had come to Earth; God had come to man.

Shepherds tending their flocks at night were given the good news by a heavenly choir. Angels heralded His arrival: "For unto you is born this day in the city of David a Saviour, which is Christ the Lord" (Lk. 2:11).

Mary, after wiping the infant clean, placed Him on her bosom. Her eyes beaming with pride looked up to Joseph as he embraced mother and child. She was ostracized; her impeccable character questioned by everyone, even those closest to her. She contributed her net worth for this to transpire, but the expense was nothing compared to the experience.

Some Greek texts imply that the cupbearer mentioned in the Old Testament had to be a eunuch, that he was not afforded earthly pleasures. His duty was to taste the wine before it reached the lips of the king. It was a precautionary measure; if the wine was poisoned, then the king lived and the cupbearer died. The positive side to performing this dangerous task was this: *He got to be in the presence of the king always.*

The Day Will Come...

No one was closer to Jesus than Mary. She was in His presence always. Her obedience and sacrifice granted her a special relationship with Christ. She enjoyed an intimacy no other would attain.

Not a day passed that she was not with Him. In the morning she plucked Him from the crib and fed Him from her own body. At evening she kissed the soft skin of His face and tucked Him in. If at any moment, day or night, she desired to hold Him, He was right there.

At times in our walk with the Lord it seems as if we have Him all to ourselves. It takes no effort to touch Him and hear His voice. At the mere whisper of His name He draws near, and we sense the gentle caress of His hand upon our shoulder. In these moments of supplication, we are enthralled in His presence.

Days spent in distress are soon forgotten within minutes of being with Him. Like fresh air after a dreadful storm, we arise with renewed strength to continue our journey.

Mary knew that one day things would drastically change. Every parent realizes the inevitable is just around the corner. James was correct when he compared life to a vapor that soon vanishes away (see Jas. 4:14). Someone once said that today we have our children on our knees, and tomorrow they will have us on our knees!

The Impassioned Soul

My wife Marilyn and I are blessed with two beautiful daughters. At times I would like to freeze these precious gals in time and not have to think of the day when they will leave to make their own home.

Marilyn chose to homeschool our oldest daughter because of my rigorous schedule. Many times I came home from a crusade and left again the next day for another. If Datha had attended a public school, I could not have spent any quality time with her.

When we moved from Louisiana to Texas, I decided to alter my itinerary, and we placed Datha in a private school. My daughter was going into the fourth grade, but to me it was like sending a toddler off to preschool.

I sat with her at the breakfast table the first morning and asked if she was certain she wanted to go to school. She assured me she was. I videotaped her walking from the house to the car with lunch box in hand and backpack strapped on her shoulders.

After pacing the floor for a good part of the day and constantly checking the clock, it finally was time to get her. I was hoping she would climb into the car and say she had a horrible time and wanted to be homeschooled again. No such luck. "Dad, I have a great teacher, and I met some neat friends," she said.

Life is full of mixed emotions. It involves receiving and returning. The time comes when we have to loosen our grip and let them experience life on their own. That gruesome day I relinquished a part of my daughter to others and knew that the process of letting go had begun.

When Kayla, our youngest daughter, started school, I had to relive the ordeal once again. Marilyn and I dropped her off and as she made her way to her classroom, I spotted tears running down Marilyn's face.

The day is approaching like a speeding freight train when they will walk across the stage and tassels will be flipped. Presently I am the only man in their lives. If the Lord tarries in His coming, young men will invade our space and request their hand in marriage.

One day a minister will ask me, "Who gives this woman in marriage?" Who gives!? I will have to practice what I have preached. In order to get I will have to give. To date my title is Dad. If I am ever going to attain the title of Granddad, it will cost me dearly. Even so come, Lord Jesus!

It seems as if it were just yesterday they were tripping over their mother's clothes playing dress-up. Tomorrow they will be changing diapers and keeping house. Knowing that change is inevitable, I savor each moment I get to spend with my two gifts from Heaven.

When Jesus was 12 years old, He gave Mary a terrible fright. Joseph had taken them to Jerusalem to pay their taxes. They were a good day into the journey home when suddenly Mary realized Jesus wasn't with them.

Horror filled Mary's face after they carefully retraced their steps and didn't find Him. They inquired in the street if anyone had seen Him. Someone passed by and mumbled something about a lad talking in the temple with lawyers and scribes. He was not only answering their questions, but also asking intriguing ones of His own.

When Mary reprimanded Him, His response was, "Wist ye not that I must be about My Father's business?" (Lk. 2:49) He made reference to His Father, reminding Mary and Joseph that there was a part of Him they could not possess (see Lk. 2:41-49).

Mary remembered the immaculate conception brought about by God, not man. She could hold Him but not have Him. She knew His day was coming, but this was much too early.

Yesterday He was a cuddly baby nestled in a manger. Now He was a robust young man assisting Joseph in the carpenter shop. Thirty years had passed so quickly.

Jesus attended a marriage supper with His mother and His disciples. As the festivities were underway, Mary announced to Him that there was no wine. The reply she received startled her: "Woman, what have I to do with thee? Mine hour is not yet come" (Jn. 2:4).

The Impassioned Soul

After 30 years of His addressing her as mother, this was totally unexpected. Had Jesus just placed the one who was partly responsible for His life in the general category of women?

The apron strings were dangling loosely. "Whatsoever He saith unto you, do it," she told the servants (Jn. 2:5). Jesus commanded the servants to fill the water pots with water and place them on the table where the governor of the feast sat. Water became wine, and Jesus began His miracle ministry (see Jn. 2:1-11).

Finally, after 30 long years, Mary received vindication. Through the span of this time, she held on to the hope that one day miracles would be performed. When they saw Him for who He was, they would see her as she really was. If anyone at the feast questioned Mary's past, the rumors were laid to rest.

She waited for this day with dread and delight. You see, He won't be coming home with Mary. When she walked past His room, His bed was unoccupied. Tomorrow morning He would not sit down with the family for breakfast, don the nail apron, and go to work in the shop.

It was not easy for her to adjust to the way things had suddenly become. All of His life He was so close, and now He seemed so terribly far away. She peered out the window, hoping to spot Him strolling down the familiar road. But it never happened.

The lame were walking, deaf were hearing, and once hopeless lepers were rejoicing, but not Mary. If He would just pay a visit, it would mean so much. After she invested 30 years of her life in Him, she just could not simply walk away and forget them.

Have you ever felt that way? "Lord, I have done all that I know to do. I have prayed, fasted, and tried desperately to be of service to You." Yet you wonder if you will ever feel His touch again. There were times in the past when it was so easy, and now, regardless how long and fervently you pray, it seems to be of no avail.

God, Remember Me?

Jesus was ministering in a town not far from Nazareth. Mary and the Lord's brothers came hoping to get an opportunity to visit with Him. When they arrived they found the building filled to capacity. "Ma'am, I am sorry, but there is absolutely no room for anyone else to squeeze through the door," explained the usher to Mary.

"Would you please tell Jesus that His mother and brothers would like to have a word with Him?" replied Mary.

The usher weaved through the mass of people captivated with the Lord's teaching. "Jesus, Your mother and brothers are outside and would like to say hello." It was not an unreasonable request. She gave Him 30 years; surely He could spare her 30 minutes.

"Who is My mother and brothers? It is those who do the will of My Father," responded Jesus. (See Matthew 12:46-50.) Those words must have pierced Mary's heart. "Who is My mother?" She suffered reproach, placed her life in jeopardy, and all but lost Joseph as a result of this scenario. Now her own Son didn't remember her. Surely she merited a little favor with Him! The person who had been on the inside was suddenly on the outside.

Perhaps you feel like you are in Mary's shoes. You watch as those who barely know Him are overwhelmed by His presence. They are experiencing a downpour of His Spirit, and you would like to have just a drop spill over onto you. People who do not profess to be Christians are instantly healed while once again you leave with excruciating pain riveting your body.

He had time for a woman caught in the act of adultery, yet didn't stop in and say hello to His mom.

A woman who had been married five times and was indulging once again in immorality got an audience with Jesus (see Jn. 4:7-30). It appeared that she was actually closer to Him than Mary was. He had time for a woman caught in the act of adultery (see Jn. 8:3-11), yet didn't stop in and say hello to His mom.

It would be easy for Mary to feel abandoned. When God required her services she was available. Now she was in need, but where was He? How many times have you shared Mary's sentiments? It's not that you want to monopolize Christ. You just so desperately need a moment with Him. You have no animosity toward the people who are rejoicing; you simply wish you had a reason to do the same.

Perhaps after a life of service for the Lord, you are experiencing a vacuum. You are exhausted after sacrificing so that others might have an opportunity to know Jesus.

You witnessed countless people receive His touch as you ministered to them. You anointed people with oil and whispered His precious name, and sickness took flight. Now you are the one afflicted.

You spent the best years of your life tramping through jungles in Third World countries spreading the gospel. Going out of your way to get there is certainly an understatement. You forged onward in spite of the fact that your own health was breaking down. A pity party is the farthest thing from your mind. Self-gratification is not your objective. You just want to be remembered.

This blood-thirsty mob was demanding that Jesus be put to death. They chose a robber over the Redeemer.

The only thing your heavenly Father forgot about you is your sin. Everything you did for His Kingdom is indelibly written in His mind. In Psalm 8:4a David asked, "What is man, that Thou art mindful of him?" Or let's put it this way: "What is man, that Your mind is full of him?"

Just Continue

Mary could not see herself rejoicing; Christ could. Remind yourself that He sees the end from the beginning. There will come a time when you will bask in the warmth of His presence. The closeness you will enjoy will be such that you have never known before. The Father has made you a promise, and God is not a man that He should lie (see Num. 23:19).

Nero estimated that there were at least three million people in Jerusalem the day Jesus stood before Pilate. This bloodthirsty mob demanded that Jesus be put to death. They chose a robber over the Redeemer. The one worthy of the death penalty was released while the spotless Lamb of God was condemned (see Mt. 27:17-25).

With a weighty cross strapped to His back, chafing against His raw flesh, He slowly made His way up Golgotha's hill. When the heavy timber forced Him to the ground, He struggled to His feet and continued (see Mk. 15:20-22; Jn. 19:17).

The brawny Roman soldiers who wielded mallets to fasten Him to the tree did not have to wrestle Him down. Willingly He stretched out on the cross and awaited His doom.

Still, His human body thrashed wildly against the cross as His nerves reacted to the inhumane punishment. Thorns pierced His temples as blood and water poured out of His side.

Eyes about to close in death opened widely. Jesus spotted Mary among the mocking masses. Enduring the scoffing and being punished unjustly were heavy weights to bear; knowing that mother was watching was too much (see Jn. 19:26).

I wonder if there were a few things Jesus would have liked to have said to Mary. "I want to thank you for being the best mother a man could ever wish for. I know that My coming into this world was not easy on you. I'm sorry that I haven't been around to see you these past few years. It must have upset you deeply when you came to visit and I asked, 'Who is My mother?' Mary, I never have and never will forget who you are. I hate that you have to see Me like this. You don't deserve to endure such agony."

The Impassioned Soul

Mary's stomach wrenched in anguish as she watched her boy hang on the tree. How could anyone who had done only right be done so wrong? She had ached to see Him again, but certainly not on these terms. John, the disciple whom Jesus loved, placed his arm gently around Mary's shoulder, pulled her close to his chest, and led her away from the gruesome scene.

Her heart, already damaged so badly, surely must have been crushed that day. Oh, but He is the healer of broken hearts.

In spite of everything she had to endure, she continued. As a maligned pregnant teenager, she continued. As the Pharisees sought for facts to condemn her, she continued. When the one closest to her questioned her virtue, she continued. After the burial of her Son, with little to go on living for, she continued.

Instead of reading how Mary spent the rest of her days lamenting over the loss of her Son, we find her rejoicing. Somehow she gathered the strength to get up and go for the promise.

On that day of feasting called Pentecost when the Holy Spirit invaded the upper room, Mary was present. She was not a broken-hearted, manic-depressed shell of a woman, bitter in spirit. She was dancing and shouting, acting a little drunk, and speaking in tongues. The One she longed so much to see had just visited her. He didn't come in person, but in Spirit (see Acts 1:13-14; 2:1-15).

You have a promise to cling to. You may have suffered verbal persecution for the stand you have taken. You easily could have gone the way of least resistance, but you chose to step out in faith and pursue what you felt to be the will of God.

You may have lost some friends along the journey, but you acquired One who will never leave you. Don't allow seeds of hatred to spring up in your heart. Love those who despitefully use you. Don't come to your own defense; let Christ be your judge.

God is not in the business of humiliating people. He came to pick you up, not to let you down. The end will justify the means. One of these days, something miraculous will occur and all will see the hand of God. There is a seat in the upper room with your name on it. Don't miss the prayer meeting. Don't give up on that church you so desperately want to see revived, on the fresh anointing that your ministry is lacking. Hold on. Continue. I feel a heavenly breeze heading your way.

When the enemy of your soul asks, "Where is Jesus?"—suggesting that the Lord has forgotten you—remember the words of Isaiah: He shall be called *Immanuel*, God with us (see Is. 7:14; Mt. 1:23).

Chapter Eight

Water

*And David longed, and said, Oh that one would give
me drink of the water of the well of Bethlehem, which
is by the gate! And the three mighty men brake through
the host of the Philistines, and drew water out of the
well of Bethlehem, that was by the gate, and took it, and
brought it to David: nevertheless he would not drink
thereof, but poured it out unto the Lord. And he said,
Be it far from me, O Lord, that I should do this: is
not this the blood of the men that went in jeopardy
of their lives? therefore he would not drink it.
These things did these three mighty men.*
2 Samuel 23:15-17

Please indulge me briefly, and let's touch on certain events in
David's life in order to lay a foundation for this chapter. By doing so
we will arrive at the main theme with better understanding of our
scriptural base. Although these events are not necessarily in their
chronological order, they illustrate a man whose heart is set on wor-
shiping his Lord.

The Protocol of Praise

If anyone ever had deep insight into praise, it was David. As a shepherd he would sit on the grassy knolls of the Judean hillside, strum his harp, and compose songs. The sound of bleating sheep mingled with soft melodic tunes drifted across the velveteen landscape. A good part of each day was spent focusing on the goodness of God with a heart full of thanksgiving.

When an unclean spirit oppressed King Saul, relief could be enjoyed only when David played for him. The irate king then would lose his temper and heave a javelin at David. The young musician, dodging the spear, would continue strumming his harp until the malicious demon was expelled (see 1 Sam. 18:10-11).

In the 73 psalms attributed to David, the word *praise* appears frequently. Many psalms begin with "Praise ye the Lord." It is David who tells us the proper procedure for entering the Lord's presence.

Make a joyful noise unto the Lord, all ye lands. Serve the Lord with gladness: come before His presence with singing. Know ye that the Lord He is God: it is He that hath made us, and not we ourselves; we are His people, and the sheep of His pasture. Enter into His gates with thanksgiving, and into His courts with praise: be thankful unto Him, and bless His name. For the Lord is good; His mercy is everlasting; and His truth endureth to all generations (Psalm 100).

As the Ark of the Covenant was returning to Jerusalem after being in obscurity at Abinadab's and then Obededom's home, David, now king of Israel, disrobed down to a loincloth and danced before the Lord with all his might. Leaping and spinning demonstratively, he welcomed the ark home. Michal, his wife, embarrassed and appalled by her husband's disgraceful behavior, called him a buffoon. His response to her rebuke was, "And I will yet be more vile than thus [for the Lord]" (2 Sam. 6:22).

David realized that the royalty and majesty of the heavenly Kingdom superseded his earthly domain. Had it not been for God, he would not be occupying the throne of Israel. After enduring a season void of God's glory, David eagerly rendered praise upon seeing it return.

David understood the protocol to praise. After he sinned by numbering Israel, the Lord presented him with three options: seven years of famine, fleeing from his enemies for three months, or three days of pestilence. David chose the latter, and 70,000 men were killed by a hideous plague. The destroying angel then stretched his hand toward Jerusalem and would have annihilated the entire population of the city, except the Lord restrained him.

The prophet Gad instructed David to erect an altar and offer sacrifice to remove the plague from Israel. The site for the oblation was the threshing floor of Araunah the Jebusite.

Araunah offered, free of charge, the threshing floor, the animal for the sacrifice, and the material needed to build the altar. David refused and explained that he could not offer unto the Lord something that had cost him nothing. He purchased the necessary items for 50 shekels of silver. (See Second Samuel 24.)

Sacrifices were not to be taken lightly. This was a holy ritual involving an offering acceptable to God. The requirements called for the best of one's flock; it was not merely an exercise in formality where anything would suffice.

David understood that he had to make good for his offense; no one else could pay his penalty. He refused to take the way of least resistance. After experiencing such carnage, being cheap was the farthest thing from David's mind.

Pleasure in Pleasing

For whosoever shall give you a cup of water to drink in My name, because ye belong to Christ, verily I say unto you, he shall not lose his reward (Mark 9:41).

The Impassioned Soul

Another snapshot we see of David is of a man reminiscing on the good things of his childhood. A special place was embedded deep within his heart for his hometown, Bethlehem. He remembered the fresh taste of the sparkling cool water he drank there as a lad. David's mouth moistened as he yearned to have another drink from the well (see 2 Sam. 23:15).

Retrieving the water was no easy task; the Philistines had laid siege to Bethlehem. In order to gain access to the well, those ungodly titans would have to be conquered. One needed to consider if water was worth engaging the enemy in battle and possibly losing one's life.

Had it been an edict issued by the king, it would have been viewed in an entirely different perspective. If orders are not obeyed, heads will roll. However, David was not demanding the water; only referring to it longingly.

David's three mighty men overheard their beloved king. They huddled and discussed the merits of his desire. If they were to pursue satisfying his craving, it most assuredly would not be a scrimmage; it was the real thing—war.

These three men were committed to protecting David at all costs—all for one, one for all. They would take an arrow for him if needed. However, David's life was not in jeopardy. The enemy had not captured the king, holding him hostage, using him as a bargaining tool so their concessions would be met.

What do you do in the case where it is not a matter of life or death? David simply desired it; he didn't demand the water. I guess the bottom line is, if one was to attempt such a dangerous feat, his motive had to be pleasing the king.

Let's look at a brief profile on each of these mighty men, rare specimens indeed.

- Adino: Talk about a man's man! This guy killed 800 men at one time. Better than that, he did it with just a spear. Wielding a sword against such a host is not something I would look forward to, but using a spear? That is totally unreasonable (see 2 Sam. 23:8).

- Eleazar: He smote the Philistines so long, his hand had to be pried from the hilt of his sword. Faithful to the end, he focused on victory and did not stop until it was attained (see 2 Sam. 23:9-10).

- Shammah: The Philistines had captured a bean patch. Everyone fled except Shammah—he stood in its midst defending it until he slew the Philistines. Regardless of the opposition and lack of support, he refused to relinquish what was his (see 2 Sam. 23:11-12).

After reviewing the pedigrees of this dynamic trio, I don't think one could ask for a more daring and dedicated group of men. Where do you find men who possess such indomitable spirits? These are not the swashbuckling Errol Flynn, Hollywood type. They were entrusted with the duty of being closest to the king in order to provide security for him at all times.

Had they existed in 1991, they would have saved the United States and the United Nations billions of dollars. Instead of commissioning well over 600,000 troops with high-tech weaponry to liberate Kuwait, we could have left the task to these men. I am confident that they would have gotten the job done.

Was it because of their genetic makeup that these men were so dauntless and victorious in battle? Being that way from birth would certainly provide a logical answer to their loyalty and integrity.

I don't think that is the case, though. Remember when David was holed up in the cave of Adullam? Four hundred men in distress, in debt, and discontent came to him—not exactly Navy Seals or the Delta Force (see 1 Sam. 22:1-2). David accepted them as they were. He never forgot where he came from. Jesse certainly never viewed David as the pick of the litter; he believed his other sons would achieve great status, but not David.

Through the years that followed, God allowed David to go through tough and trying times. These incidents developed character in David—and not only him, but also in 400 men who previously did not know what it was like to enjoy a good night's rest and hold down a job.

Frayed nerves and inflamed ulcers were their life stories. Talk about a metamorphosis! They were changed from mice into men; from zeroes into heroes. Out of those 400 despondent losers emerged three intrepid men who would go to any length to please their king, even if it meant losing their life.

Many will do only what they are made or paid to do. If it is an absolute order with no alternative, they will grudgingly do what is expected and nothing extra. When the consequences could be fatal, volunteers are exceptionally rare.

Out of those 400 despondent losers emerged three intrepid men who would go to any length to please their king, even if it meant losing their life.

The Philistines, known for their height, strength, and competence in battle, have historically proved to be a worthy foe. Three courageous comrades drew their swords from their scabbards and entered intense combat with the adversary.

They are not on a conquest for the holy grail or to free the king. Their objective was to subdue the enemy and gain access to the well. If flesh wounds were suffered or if one fell to the ground, it was a price that must be paid.

War was not the only job description for these men. Adino, Eleazar, and Shammah occupied prestigious positions and moved in popular circles. When David made public appearances, these three valiant soldiers were visible to his subjects. With sabers glistening and medals shining, they accompanied the king down the red carpet to the throne.

The reason they enjoyed nearly unlimited access to David was their allegiance and their willingness to accomplish any task, whether great or small. Most are available only if the danger is minimal and the reward sufficient.

If one only knew the reward in being a water boy! If only we realized the value in striving to acquire something that is free, yet could be costly to attain; in making oneself available for whatever the task might be; in possessing the willingness to serve in whatever capacity might be required.

Many years ago in a small town in Louisiana, a teenage boy walked to church. When he arrived, the saints were standing outside the sanctuary with no way to get in. The deacon who was responsible for unlocking the doors was at home sick in bed. There was no phone available to call the deacon and no car to drive to his house.

It appeared as though the church service would have to be canceled. The young teenage boy volunteered to run the two miles—one way—to the deacon's house and get the key.

If one only knew the reward in being a water boy. If only we realized the value in striving to acquire something that is free, yet could be costly to attain....

Exhausted, the boy returned and slipped the key into the lock. As the door was opening, the Lord spoke to the lad. *Because you have done this, I have placed into your hand the key to lead this church.* We knew him as George Glass, Sr., former pastor of the First Pentecostal Church of Derrider, Louisiana.

This man was known as one of the greatest preachers of our time. Conferences and camp meetings were blessed on numerous occasions by his ministry. Many of George Glass's sermons are still remembered to this day as if they were preached just yesterday.

Many people have misconstrued ideas about the ministry because of televangelists. They see televangelists as having the same status as a movie star. This is not to indict anyone who chooses to utilize the media to propagate the gospel or to slam a professionally produced religious program. I am of the opinion that whatever we do for the Lord should be done with excellence.

I am not opposed to ministering via multimedia. We must reach the lost at any cost. I am dealing with the by-product: What do the viewers perceive the ministry to be?

The ministry has nothing to do with popularity but everything to do with being a servant. The minister who officiated at my ordination handed me a towel, saying, "I hand you a towel rather than a scepter. Always remember that you have been called to be a servant."

Jesus Christ Himself stooped to wash the dusty feet of the disciples. When Peter attempted to stop the Lord, Jesus replied, "If I wash thee not, thou hast no part with Me" (Jn. 13:8c).The revelation of serving illuminated Peter's heart: "Lord, not my feet only, but also my hands and my head" (Jn. 13:9b).

Is it the limelight that impresses you in being one of the king's mighty men? If you can appear in public but not in battle, then are you willing to apply for the position? Are you too big to tackle small chores? Does the thought of fetching water dampen your desire? After all, mighty men shouldn't have to mess with such trivial tasks. You want to be used in the gifts of the Spirit, but are you willing to teach a Bible study or simply to unlock the door? Before you lay hands on the sick, you may be asked to offer helping hands to someone in need.

Christ did not say that if He could not lay hands on our heads we could not have any part of His Kingdom. But He did say that He must wash our feet. Not all are called to heal, but all are called to serve. Sometimes ordinary men do extraordinary things. The question is, can extraordinary men do ordinary things?

The person whom God wants to use is someone who will meet not only demands but also desires. Such a one does not require a direct order to motivate him; the merest hint from Heaven suffices.

The slogan of the U.S. Marine Corps is, "We need a few good men." How can the Church of Jesus Christ increase the number of willing participants? A mandatory draft cannot be enforced. God doesn't work that way.

Yet our mission is so much more crucial than vanquishing a tyrant and restoring democracy in a hostile nation. Egomaniacs and power hungry people need not apply. We need a few brave souls who will not cower in a crisis.

The supreme need of the hour is for someone to place a finger on the pulse of Heaven and find out what God desires. Commitments, not commandments, are needed to mobilize the Church. "I have to" will be replaced with "I get to" when pleasing Christ becomes paramount.

We must seek to find our respective positions in the Body of Christ. Whether we are an eye, ear, or just a tiny blood vessel, we must serve in that capacity. When saints get a revelation of the blessings in doing small things, the number of volunteers will reach an all-time high, prayer rooms will be packed, and church attendance will increase substantially.

Helping When Hurting

The widow of Zarephath in First Kings 17 made the funeral arrangements. She knew that soon the biers would be laden with her corpse, as well as her son's. Their last meal would consist of a single cake, and then they would succumb to death. The grim reaper was quickly becoming a welcome guest, due to their dire circumstances. The gruesome sight of watching her boy starve before her eyes was too much to endure. And malnutrition was taking its toll on her as well.

For three and a half years an unrelenting famine had plagued the land. The sizzling rays of the sun scorched her back; the molten clay beneath blistered her feet. No sign of green vegetation could be seen—just the charred remnants of what used to be.

The incinerating temperature coupled with not a single drop of rain had extinguished the agriculture industry. Streams and rivers that previously flowed with shimmering, rapid water merged into the arid desert panorama.

The ingredients for the final supper are as simple as the utensils for cooking it. Picking up two sticks to prepare the oil and meal, the widow noticed a stranger approaching. His pace was swift, and it did not appear that he had missed any meals of late.

"Ma'am, could I please have a cup of water?" requested the stranger. If anyone here was in need, she was the one, not this sojourner who must have had a secret supply of food stowed away. Yet he had the audacity to ask from her, when her plight was so obvious.

But this was no ordinary stranger; it was the preacher she had been hearing about. The wickedness of King Ahab and his diabolical wife Jezebel prompted Elijah to prophesy a draught into existence. The pagan practices of heathenized royalty rendered the judgment of God upon a nation. Righteous people were affected as well as the unrighteous.

What was the big deal about water, anyway? The answer is that if she responded without reacting, she would secure for today a tomorrow that never existed.

This was not the most convenient time to ask this widow for a favor. I would not think it unselfish of her if she had been the one soliciting good will. Perhaps God was testing her to see if she would give when she should be getting. She was on the brink of her blessing, but the question was, how would she respond to the prophet's request?

It would have been so easy to give Elijah a piece of her mind, to fire both barrels and tell him like it is. How could anyone possibly be so inconsiderate? Life would go on for him. The future for her and her son was vanishing faster than a snowflake in hell.

What was the big deal about water, anyway? The answer is that if she responded without reacting, she would secure for today a tomorrow that never existed. Funeral plans would be canceled, the boy would become a man, and the famine would be robbed of claiming some more victims.

She obliged the prophet, and the law of cause and effect was set in motion. The first domino was jostled, and everything else fell into place. Wow! How close did she actually come to blowing it? It would have been so easy to think of her son's need instead of the preacher's (see 1 Kings 17:9-15).

Weary Yet Willing

The day was spent and long monotonous hours of arduous chores were finally over, at least for today. In the morning Rebekah would awaken and repeat the routine. Now it was evening, and only one detail remained: fetching water for the house.

Balancing a pitcher on her shoulder, Rebekah set out on her final task. In the dusk she noticed a man sitting alongside the well with several camels kneeling around him.

When she stepped outside her home, her intentions had been simple. She had absolutely no idea that she was approaching a date with destiny. Her simple mundane life was being interrupted by God, and she would experience a transformation unlike anything she had ever dreamed (see Gen. 24:10-19).

Talk about a transition! She was nearing the perimeter that encompassed notoriety and greatness. That very day was spent as all the rest before it, performing trivial tasks. She was not anticipating anything outstanding to occur. Little did she realize that history would record her as the matriarch of patriarchs—if, while being weary, she was still willing.

Once again we find a man asking water from a woman. The widow of Zarephath had lost her husband; Rebekah had yet to find hers. The missing element in both of their lives was asking for something.

The man had been sitting at the well for some time. Wouldn't it seem logical that he should help himself if he was really that thirsty? The consistency here seems to be that God is interested in our attitude. Whether we are on the edge of extinction or ambling faithfully through life (even though things may never become brighter), when our moment of visitation arrives, how will we respond?

When asked for water, Rebekah replied, "Yes, I will draw water for you—as well as for your camels." Oh! There are ten camels—each one of which can consume 20 gallons—and Rebekah just offered to draw water for them until they finish drinking! If these camels were registering on empty, she had just created a laborious job for herself (see Gen. 24:10-19).

Be careful when you need a hand up and you're asked for a handout.

She was fully aware that her brow would sweat and her back ache; nevertheless, she offered anyhow. Her immediate plans to carry water to the house and relax in a soothing bath would be delayed. Weary from the day's labor, Rebekah began working overtime.

Life would never be the same for this virtuous woman. Her faithfulness initiated the plan of God in her life. She would go from carrying water to bearing babies. Being willing at evening made way for a new day to dawn—a day different from any other.

Be careful when you need a hand up and you're asked for a handout. If you are suddenly placed in the position to serve, don't react in bitterness. Perhaps life has not been treating you fairly, and now, as if your duties are not enough, another one is shoved before you. How will you react?

God never creates a task too great for us to accomplish. You may be a single mom because of a delinquent dad who never could deal with responsibility. Perhaps you are left to finish the race alone since your beloved has gone on before you. Whatever the situation, be willing. If a need arises, be there and be willing.

You may have gone through more marriages than an accountant has numbers. The chap you are living with at the moment takes what he wants but will not give you his name in return. His free spirit and fear of commitment will not permit him to enter into a marriage contract. These irresponsible, poor excuses of the male gender may have disillusioned you, but the Man sitting at your well is different. If you will give Him what He asks, He will give you what you need.

It is not that drawing water is a dangerous or momentous task. However, it could be the catalyst that decides your future. As you have already perceived, providing water is a figure of speech. The bottom line is to make yourself available for whatever is placed in front of you.

Whatsoever thy hand findeth to do, do it with thy might (Ecclesiastes 9:10a).

Water Too Good for a King

With swords clashing and sweat mingled with blood dripping to the ground, three mighty men broke through enemy lines. Lowering the pail into the well, Adino, Eleazar, and Shammah retrieved the water their king was longing to taste.

The dreadful and perhaps almost fatal combat was soon forgotten as they approached David. Their hearts were elated in pleasing the king; thus the reason for forgetting the battle.

"I cannot drink this," the king exclaimed. David was humbled to such a degree that he would not drink the water. "But, king, why not? It has already been tested by your cupbearer." David replied, "It's not that I fear it is poisoned; it is too good for me to drink. This is the blood of you who put your lives in jeopardy" (see 2 Sam. 23:17).

The man who had understanding of praise and worship and who was fully aware of the requirements in offering an acceptable sacrifice unto God, poured the water out unto the Lord.

He was not fearful of presenting something unworthy; he knew the price these men paid. It was not frankincense, myrrh, or costly perfume; it was not vintage wine that sat in a cellar aging to perfection. It was simply water.

Enormous value was added to the water because of the willingness of these men to acquire it. It was water too good for an earthly king, but acceptable for the King of kings.

Perfect Praise

All week you have been engaged in a fierce conflict with the enemy of your soul. Just keeping your spirit right, your tongue silent, and your mind clean has left you battle-weary. Everything that can go wrong has, and then some.

With funds shrinking and bills accumulating, you continue struggling to make ends meet. Although your present job is undesirable, you punch the clock and put in another day. Returning home with feet nearly swollen out of your shoes, you slump into a chair and wonder if it is worth it.

Tonight is a church night, but that bed sure looks inviting. After all, who will see that you are missing? You don't sing in the choir or play the keyboard. It is not your responsibility to stand behind the pulpit and deliver the sermon. The most you do is sit, listen, and "amen" the preacher. Your offering is the kind that makes a noise when dropped into the basket. It sure would be nice to be in the position to give 20 dollars instead of 20 cents.

Your voice is not compatible with the choir. Your contributions to the service are minimal at best. Why not just stay home? But you can't. It is not that you think the service cannot go on without you; it's just that something inside you will not permit you to miss.

Thinking that tonight will be like any other service, you make your way to church. With hands raised high and your mouth opened wide rendering praise, Heaven descends upon you. Weariness of body and cares of life vanish as you weep with gratitude in being allowed another opportunity to be in the Lord's presence.

As the glory of God intensifies, you wish that you had something special to offer Him. The best you can do is to stand and humbly whisper praises. You see, what you think to be minute, God deems magnanimous. The praises that issue from your heart have come before God as a sweet-smelling savor.

You're offering water, if you please. When no one else was aware of your struggles, God was watching. He saw you fighting to maintain your sanity when the world was collapsing around you. When you teetered on the precipice of despair, you somehow regained your footing and kept on standing.

When giants of discouragement tried to prevent you from nearing the well, you persevered. The words of thanksgiving on your lips did not get there easily. You fought hell and high water to bring them to the house of God. There were times when you came close to losing them, but when tempted to complain, you opted to praise.

Now you understand why the devil had you in his crosshairs. He knew that your heavenly King desired water, so he surrounded the well. But you prevailed. It may be a simple "hallelujah" that you offer to Him. It is more than a few syllables, though; it is pleasure to your King.

When you teetered on the precipice of despair, you somehow regained your footing and kept on standing.

There is no need to feel inadequate because of your lack of talent. You may not be capable of carrying a tune in a bucket, but go ahead and sing anyway. You most likely will never be issued an invitation to perform in Carnegie Hall, but your song has made the charts in Heaven.

The Impassioned Soul

It is easy to sing a tune on a clear day at noon. You are singing in the proverbial midnight of your life. As the rain keeps pouring and the wind keeps blowing, you keep singing. Every note, whether on key or off, echoes through the jasper walls of glory. Angelic choirs are silent; harps are refrained from playing as all of Heaven savors the sweet fragrance of your praise.

Chapter Nine

Snow

*Hast thou entered into the treasures of the snow? or
hast thou seen the treasures of the hail, which I have
reserved against the time of trouble, against the day
of battle and war?*
Job 38:22-23

In the kitchen window of a modest two-story house in Black's Harbor, New Brunswick, Canada, several faces pressed against the glass playing "car conquer." I have absolutely no idea how we ever came up with this name, but this is how we played: By the hour we would sit staring out the window watching for our older brothers and sisters to arrive home for Christmas. Some lived a thousand miles away, so it was very exciting to see them again, especially at this time of year. We would try to guess if it were their car coming down the road. That's pretty much the gist of it. Not exactly Jeopardy, but it generated a lot of fun.

Between working at the factory, attending church, and raising her family, Mother took time to bake plenty of delicious sweets in advance. I would stand at the table salivating, watching her roll her famous molasses cookies. I loved dipping them in a cold glass of milk, but getting one before it reached the oven was a special treat. Turkey, dressing, cranberry sauce, and homemade apple pie comprised the Christmas dinner. It was a meal fit for a king, and we all were aware how hard our parents worked to provide it for us.

Winter evenings would find us snuggled around the oil heater in our living room. The ultimate comfort zone was getting to sit next to the heater and prop your feet on the door. Many a battle was waged to acquire this envied spot. I can still see Mother sitting there knitting woolen socks and mittens.

The Christmas program at our church featured a rhythm band. There was no auditioning to see who would play what. Whoever got to the music chest first selected their favorite instrument. I always wanted to get my hands on the plastic guitar, but I usually ended up with something less desirable.

Each child who attended the Christmas concert was handed a bag of candy from their Sunday school teacher, which usually held two or three chocolates along with some hardtack. The chocolates were eaten before any other piece. If not, my older brothers enjoyed them without my having a taste. You can imagine the atmosphere at our house when that happened.

Listening to Bing Crosby singing "I'll Be Home for Christmas" never fails to cause a lump in my throat and a tear in my eye as I reminisce of the big family in the little house at Christmas time. Presents were not expensive, but the warmth of family made up for any deficit.

There is something very special about the first snowfall of the season. We children eagerly awaited its arrival, sometimes fearing that we would not have any for Christmas. While the record on the phonograph played Elvis singing "I'll Have a Blue Christmas," we feared having a green Christmas.

I recall a few years when it appeared that we would have no snow. We could not imagine having Christmas without snow. Then our fears vanished as huge fluffy flakes gracefully drifted down and piled on top of each other, covering the ground.

Another fond memory of winter is the snow sculptures our local high school students created. Everything from igloos, snowmobiles, and Snoopy were entered into the contest.

Sometimes the temperature would fall to -40° Fahrenheit, and yet we still were not content to stay indoors. My siblings and I donned our coats, mittens, and caps and headed for the nearest hill. On over-crowded toboggans we slid down the slope, the girls screeching all the way to the bottom. Grudgingly, we took turns pulling the sled back to the top.

With snow shovels and makeshift plows, we cleared the snow off a frozen lake—a process that sometimes took hours. Then the quiet-ness of a peaceful Saturday morning was shattered with the shouts of names borrowed from the National Hockey League. I don't remember anyone who played with us having the potential to turn professional, but we all had plenty of zeal.

Hardly a one of us had the proper protective equipment. From experience I can tell you that a hard puck striking you on the kneecap can warm up your cold carcass in a hurry. One minute you fear frost-bite; the next you feel heat shoot from your head down to your toes.

Several times upon leaving the ice at early evening, I promised myself that I would not participate in such torture again. With freez-ing feet and numb fingertips, I meandered off the ice—only to return for the next game.

When winter came, some loathed it while others loved it. How-ever, even the ones who avidly participated in winter sports grew weary of the cold weather and snow. Defrosting windshields, negoti-ating treacherous driving conditions, and constantly tracking slush through homes and cars can spoil the fun in winter. It is one thing to live in a warm climate year-round and fly somewhere for a ski trip.

That way you can take it or leave it. When you have to endure it for several months, it becomes monotonous rather than convenient.

For us there was no escaping this season of life. We had to live with it, so we opted to enjoy it. Few, if any, of the people we knew enjoyed the luxury of heading south to sandy beaches. At times Old Man Winter settled in with his twin brother Jack Frost, and together they released their frigid breath, freezing everything solid, suggesting that they were here to stay. Still, we knew that sooner or later they would pack up and leave, bumping into springtime as they left.

Winter is not a medieval torture chamber invented to punish those living in areas affected by its subzero temperatures and waist-deep snow. Like everything else created by God, winter serves a purpose. The snow that is warmly welcomed and soon despised possesses a treasure.

Pray, No Matter the Season

California is the United States' leading agricultural producer. This western state exceeds every other in approximately 50 crop commodities. In some specialty crop markets, California is the sole domestic source.

This is not due to the annual rainfall in California, since four-fifths of its cropland is irrigated. The Colorado Desert, located in southeastern California, sometimes experiences temperatures of up to 130°F with an annual rainfall that averages three to four inches.

Some of the substantial providers of water for California's irrigation system are the snowcaps. Reservoirs collect water from the melting snow and store it for future use.

As a child of God, you will experience winter seasons in your Christian walk. You quite possibly may be there now. It's neither time to plant nor time to reap. Your rose garden has become frozen tundra. Dark brown topsoil, rich with nutrients, has become permafrost.

What is one supposed to do in the dead of winter? Consistency must be kept in every season of life. It is imperative that you maintain your prayer life, although it is not the fruit-bearing season.

Also, make sure that the farm equipment is in top running condition. Yank the engine out of the combine and replace the push rod that has been knocking, threatening to bust the engine block. Feed and care for the livestock that will populate your pastures with offspring.

The spring planting season is inevitable, warm days of summer enjoyable, and fall harvest probable, so get ready. Neglecting preparation in this season will negate production next season.

The spring planting season is inevitable, warm days of summer enjoyable, and fall harvest probable, so get ready. Neglecting preparation this season will negate production next season.

Pray without ceasing (1 Thessalonians 5:17).

At times we feel as if our prayers do not ascend beyond the ceiling above our head, but this is not the case. When we pray the will and Word of God, every prayer is answered. This statement is the cornerstone of this chapter.

"Pray without ceasing." The admonition here is not that one pray 24 hours, 7 days a week. It would be an impossible task for many people to engage in intercessory prayer while at work with the types of jobs they have. We cannot shirk our responsibilities in life and survive. Paul is encouraging us to pray and not be discouraged. In other words, pray until it happens.

Regardless of how the enemy tries to discourage you from praying, badgering you with doubt and unbelief, continue to make your petition known. When ferocious winds of opposition are howling, hold firmly to the promises of God's Word and refuse to let go.

For all the promises of God in Him are yea, and in Him Amen, unto the glory of God by us (2 Corinthians 1:20).

...yea, let God be true, but every man a liar... (Romans 3:4).

In times past when you prayed, rain came pouring down in torrents. Fire from Heaven fell, consuming the sacrifice and bringing vindication to your cause. Gusts of wind blew into your upper room, filling you with power and unspeakable joy.

Now as you pray, there is not a drop of rain, spark of fire, or enough breeze to alter the flight of a feather. But it's snowing, and perhaps you're complaining, thinking God isn't responding. There is victory in every season of life; you just must work with what God gives you.

Job implied that the treasure in the snow is reserved for the day of battle (see Job 38:22-23). God knows that somewhere in life you will be engaged in spiritual warfare. Drought will threaten to destroy your crops. Something totally unexpected will suddenly confront you, not allowing any time for prayer. You are going to need an emergency survival kit to make it. This is the treasure of the snow.

A rose bloomed in your arid desert. A fountain penetrated from beneath the concrete floor of your wilderness, providing sustenance for life's journey. As you stood with mouth agape, luxuriating in the brilliant leaves of fall, God knew that you needed a winter to endure your summer.

Summers are not always filled with fun. The summer of 1998 will go down in the history books as one of Texas's hottest. One man made a joke by calling it God's cookout, gotten out of hand. On September 20 the *Dallas Morning News* reported that, in Texas, there were 37 heat-related deaths and 29 consecutive days with temperatures in the triple digits.

The soaring temperatures mixed with dense humidity made life almost unbearable in the Lone Star state. Charitable organizations along with businesses supplied fans to residents in need. For some they came too late. One older gentleman waited in his mobile home for the air conditioning repairman to come. When he arrived, the man had already succumbed to the relentless heat.

Dryness took its toll on livestock and agriculture. Millions of gallons of drinking water were donated to alleviate thirst. Warnings not to be outside for very long periods of time were aired frequently. Watering lawns was permitted on only specified days.

It was common to see overheated automobiles parked along the shoulder of highways. In heavy traffic, tempers as well as temperatures were extremely hot, making life even more miserable.

One day I attempted to tee the ball at one of our local golf courses. The earth beneath the grass was baked so hard, it was almost like asphalt. Needless to say, this was one of the few golf outings I attempted under these conditions.

Water in the Desert

"Pray without ceasing." Pray in spite of no rain, wind, or fire. Whatever you do, don't curse the snow. Winter's wrath may have canceled important duties and obligations; life may have come to a screeching halt due to the accumulating snow. Just bundle up nice and cozy, prop your feet on the hearth, and sip on some hot chocolate.

While others experience failing crops and dying cattle, your farm is operating just fine. You prayed without ceasing in every season. Reservoirs today are full of water that melted from yesterday's storm. You are fruitful in summer because you were faithful in winter.

Your checkbook is in the red; your business is limping toward Chapter Eleven. An accident occurred, and midday has suddenly become midnight; your child is in the back of an ambulance being rushed to the hospital. You make a 911 call to Heaven. Rivers of glory flow into your life with miracles caught in their rushing current.

How is it possible that a river is flowing in your desert? The breath of God swept across a mountaintop and melted a snow-cap. Somewhere in the past you prayed a prayer you thought went unanswered. You could not see any form of precipitation—be it rain, sleet, or snow—yet you continued to pray.

While hell is raging and Heaven appears silent, whisper a prayer. Your answer is not denied, just delayed.

You looked in every direction for a sign, but nothing caught your eye. When the earth all around you lay dry and barren, snow was gathering atop mountains. When you pray the will and Word of God, every prayer is answered.

You presently may be travailing for a loved one. Thoughts of doubt assail you like flies swarming over a dead carcass; fend them off and continue to intercede. While hell is raging and Heaven appears silent, whisper a prayer. Your answer is not denied, just delayed.

And Abraham said unto God, O that Ishmael might live before Thee! (Genesis 17:18)

Abraham interceded for his son Ishmael, asking God to sustain his life. A couple of years later that teenage boy would encounter the grim reaper in the wilderness of Beersheba. With his tongue thick and throat raw from begging for water, a death rattle was detected in his voice.

Ishmael's mother, Hagar, had reached her wits' end. Like every mother, she wanted the best for her son. Being a handmaid, she knew it was not possible to bequeath upon the lad the things she desired him to have. She at least has been confident that Abraham would provide something for the future for Ishmael. But there was an obstacle that could not be hurdled: Abraham's wife Sarah. No longer would she tolerate Ishmael mocking her son Isaac. Hagar and Ishmael were ousted from the tent, and now they face imminent death.

With the water bottle empty and her nerves inflamed, Hagar did something she thought she would never do. She laid Ishmael under a shrub and began to walk away from the dearest thing to her on earth: her own flesh and blood. She was not a negligent mom; there was nothing too great for her to do for Ishmael. The terrible fact was, she could not provide something as simple and inexpensive as water.

It was not supposed to end that way. Every parent dreams of their children growing up and becoming successful in life, not dying in a desert while still a teenager. Just before the lad was snatched prematurely from life by the cadaverous hands of death, a well was spotted. The memorial prayer of Abraham spared the life of Ishmael (see Gen. 21:14-19).

Treasure in the Snow

I will ever be indebted to my dear mother and her unwavering walk with God. The little lady with a big heart whispered prayers that reverberated through the jasper walls of glory. I cannot recall mother praying with a loud voice; it wasn't her style. However, Heaven heard, and Heaven answered.

In the short time I have been living on this planet, I too have experienced dry periods in life. Just before drought claimed my harvest and dehydration my life, flood tides of blessing swept me from the banks of despair. I am a strong advocate for maintaining a personal devotion to God; however, I am quite sure that my mother's persistence on her knees many times kept me on my feet.

> *Just before the drought claimed my harvest and dehydration my life, flood tides of blessing swept me from the banks of despair.*

I remember looking at our house from across the harbor at nighttime and seeing Mother's bedroom light on. I knew it was not because she was afraid of the dark. While I was running the roads, she was kneeling beside her bed speaking the name of each of her children in prayer.

I especially remember a time in my life when I went through an experimental period. I no longer wanted to be excluded from things I deemed to be fun. Mother rarely preached to me, but she never compromised her convictions by allowing me to participate in sin in her house. Rather than remind me of what I already knew, she prayed. At approximately five o'clock one morning, while attending a party, a net of conviction was cast over me. I knew that Mother's prayers had reached the throne of God, and it was time to mend my ways.

Through the process and time of writing this book, some changes occurred. It was obvious that Mother was about to be promoted. At the time mother was suspended between two worlds. As angels waited to usher her home, we her family could not bear to see her go.

The nurses who lovingly tended to Mother were at first shocked when they entered her room and found so many people gathered around her bed. They were even more shocked when they learned these were all her children!

Sometimes there was a little jockeying for position as each child attempted to get their turn to be next to Mother. No wonder. I cannot adequately express how wonderful it felt to be close to Mother. To caress her hand and see her smile literally touched my heart. I file these priceless pictures in my mind and keep them as timeless treasures.

When we said our last good-bye to Mother, there was no executor brought in to divide the estate. Reading her last testament did not require much time. There were no bonds, stocks, and properties to be split among her children. Mother did not amass a fortune in this life, but she certainly does not hang her head in shame in the next.

Nevertheless, I am an heir to a fortune. You cannot place monetary value on prayer. There are too many times to mention when she prayed and seemingly never received an answer. Yet she prayed. I bear witness to the fact that most of Mother's life was lived in winter. There just were not many seasons for her that produced bumper crops and golden sunlit days.

It is here that I want to thank this godly woman for the treasure she gave to me. Whenever a snowflake drifts silently through the air, it will remind me of her prayers. Mom, thanks for the snow. I have trekked through blazing deserts and drunk from oases provided by your prayers.

A word of encouragement to all moms, dads, and grandparents: Keep on praying. When it seems that the heavens above are brass and you have not so much as heard a whisper, continue praying. Tomorrow's drought may be the reason for today's delay. Buy your children and grandchildren a present today, and they will forget about it tomorrow. Pray for them today, and they will treasure it forever. And, oh yes: Let it snow, let it snow, let it snow!

Books to help you grow strong in Jesus

▬ SECRET SOURCES OF POWER

by T.F. Tenney with Tommy Tenney.
Everyone is searching for power. People are longing for some external force to empower their lives and transform their circumstances. *Secret Sources of Power* furnishes some of the keys that will unlock the door to Divine power. You might be surprised at what is on the other side of that door. It will be the opposite of the world's concepts of power and how to obtain it. You will discover that before you lay hold of God's power you must let go of your own resources. You will be challenged to go down before you can be lifted up. Death always comes before resurrection. If you are dissatisfied with your life and long for the power of God to be manifested in you then now is the time. Take the keys and open the door to *Secret Sources of Power*!
ISBN 0-7684-5000-4

▬ THE GOD CHASERS (National Best-Seller)

by Tommy Tenney.
There are those so hungry, so desperate for His presence, that they become consumed with finding Him. Their longing for Him moves them to do what they would otherwise never do: Chase God. But what does it really mean to chase God? Can He be "caught"? Is there an end to the thirsting of man's soul for Him? Meet Tommy Tenney—God chaser. Join him in his search for God. Follow him as he ignores the maze of religious tradition and finds himself, not chasing God, but to his utter amazement, caught by the One he had chased.
ISBN 0-7684-2016-4
Also available in Spanish
ISBN 0-7899-0642-2

▬ GOD CHASERS DAILY MEDITATION & PERSONAL JOURNAL

by Tommy Tenney.
ISBN 0-7684-2040-7

▬ GOD'S FAVORITE HOUSE

by Tommy Tenney.
The burning desire of your heart can be fulfilled. God is looking for people just like you. He is a Lover in search of a people who will love Him in return. He is far more interested in you than He is interested in a building. He would hush all of Heaven's hosts to listen to your voice raised in heartfelt love songs to Him. This book will show you how to build a house of worship within, fulfilling your heart's desire and His!
ISBN 0-7684-2043-1

▬ THE LOST PASSIONS OF JESUS

by Donald L. Milam, Jr.
What motivated Jesus to pursue the cross? What inner strength kept His feet on the path laid before Him? Time and tradition have muted the Church's knowledge of the passions that burned in Jesus' heart, but if we want to—if we dare to—we can still seek those same passions. Learn from a close look at Jesus' own life and words and from the writings of other dedicated followers the passions that enflamed the Son of God and changed the world forever!
ISBN 0-9677402-0-7

Available at your local Christian bookstore.

For more information and sample chapters, visit www.reapernet.com

Destiny Image titles
you will enjoy reading

— THE POWER OF BROKENNESS
by Don Nori.
Accepting Brokenness is a must for becoming a true vessel of the Lord, and is a stepping-stone to revival in our hearts, our homes, and our churches. Brokenness alone brings us to the wonderful revelation of how deep and great our Lord's mercy really is. Join this companion who leads us through the darkest of nights. Discover the *Power of Brokenness.*
ISBN 1-56043-178-4

— HIS MANIFEST PRESENCE
by Don Nori.
This is a passionate look at God's desire for a people with whom He can have intimate fellowship. Not simply a book on worship, it faces our triumphs as well as our sorrows in relation to God's plan for a dwelling place that is splendid in holiness and love.
ISBN 0-914903-48-9
Also available in Spanish.
ISBN 1-56043-079-6

— SECRETS OF THE MOST HOLY PLACE
by Don Nori.
Here is a prophetic parable you will read again and again. The winds of God are blowing, drawing you to His Life within the Veil of the Most Holy Place. There you begin to see as you experience a depth of relationship your heart has yearned for. This book is a living, dynamic experience with God!
ISBN 1-56043-076-1

— ENCOUNTERING THE PRESENCE
by Colin Urquhart.
What is it about Jesus that, when we encounter Him, we are changed? When we encounter the Presence, we encounter the Truth, because Jesus is the Truth. Here Colin Urquhart, best-selling author and pastor in Sussex, England, explains how the Truth changes facts. Do you desire to become more like Jesus? The Truth will set you free!
ISBN 0-7684-2018-0

Available at your local Christian bookstore.